Power of Sage

Power of Sage

An Antithesis to Machiavellian Prince

Waqas M. Awan

 FIRST HILL BOOKS

FIRST HILL BOOKS
An imprint of Wimbledon Publishing Company
www.anthempress.com

This edition first published in UK and USA 2024
by FIRST HILL BOOKS
75–76 Blackfriars Road, London SE1 8HA, UK
or PO Box 9779, London SW19 7ZG, UK
and
244 Madison Ave #116, New York, NY 10016, USA

British Library Cataloguing-in-Publication Data
A catalogue record for this book is available from the British Library.

Library of Congress Cataloging-in-Publication Data: 2024901760
A catalog record for this book has been requested.

ISBN-13: 978-1-83999-213-1 (Hbk)
ISBN-10: 1-83999-213-1 (Hbk)

ISBN-13: 978-1-83999-214-8 (Pbk)
ISBN-10: 1-83999-214-X (Pbk)

This title is also available as an e-book.

CONTENTS

Part IV: Power Struggle

Part V: Power and Morality

FIGURES

MOTIVATION

The primary motivation to author the book is to propose a 4th school on how power is constructed. The book aims to give an alternative version of power. A version which is in stark contrast to the concepts put forward by Niccolo Machiavelli and in contemporary discourse championed by Henry Kissinger and Robert Greene. The general idea that power is somehow garnered through trickery, deceit and cunningness is not only medieval but also does not comply with modern ethical and moral standards. A new and modern approach to studying power is the requirement of the day, which takes away power from the old school and leads to a new understanding of power.

The hypothesis put forward by Machiavelli that a Prince should be decisive but not necessarily ethical is refuted vehemently by the concept of Sage who is not driven by survival and self-preservation but by ideology and beliefs. The motivation to write the book is to parallel the realist school of thought with the idealistic school of thought. Hopefully, by doing so, the masses will be better able to distinguish their leaders and a better leadership will emerge where humanity can become a top priority than power. We may finally see the day where the end does not justify the means.

AUTHOR'S NOTE

All the funds raised from the sale of this book are going to be diverted towards funding scholarships for deserving students of my alma mater, Ghulam Ishaq Khan Institute (GIKI). GIKI is a premiere institute in Pakistan, but due to its high tuition fee, many deserving students fail to finance their studies there. I came from a privileged background which enabled me to get an education in GIKI, but not many are as privileged as me. Since 2020, I have been helping the GIKI Alumni Association to raise funds for scholarships. As a written commitment to all my readers, I will divert all profits from this book towards the GIKI scholarship fund. The idea is to create an endowment fund so multiple students can be financed each year to get an education in GIKI.

Additionally, I request caution while reading the book. The book takes the readers through several models and segregates people and society into different categories. These models and categorizations are not mutually exclusive. A normal human and societal behaviour is not binary; rather, it comprises a spectrum of behaviour. Hence, firmly putting someone in one basket should be avoided while reading and analysing the models presented in the book. Also, the examples and thesis presented in the book may come across as perfect and a neat fit into the frameworks. This is neither the case nor the intention. No example is absolute and perfectly fits into the boundaries of the given framework. Human nature and societies always display nuance and diversity, and there will always be an exception to the rules presented in the book. The thesis of the book has been developed so as to simplify the understanding of complexity surrounding human societies rather than to give an absolute framework that is supposed to work in every situation.

Furthermore, it is assumed that the reader has some background knowledge of the event in question while citing many historical examples in the book. I have intentionally avoided giving great details as I firmly believe that the human attention span is shrinking with the advent of technology. If the information is not bite-sized, the readers lose focus. Hence, to keep the book concise, great care has been taken to use case studies which are known widely. Every chapter starts with a real-life example of a historical event and poses a question to the readers. It then cites works of great philosophers to build a theory, framework and model behind it before answering the question posed to the reader at the start of the chapter. If the reader is unaware of the case study discussed in the chapter or the philosophical work cited, in that case I recommend any online resource to study the details to get better understanding of the underlying example.

DEDICATION

The book is dedicated to the loving memory of my father, who died on 10th August 2020 without knowing that his son was authoring a book.

He was the most courageous person I met in my life.

RIP
Zafar Iqbal Awan
1943–2020

ACKNOWLEDGEMENTS

First, I would like to thank the love of my life Asma and my heartbeats, Abdullah and Uzair, for their support and encouragement throughout the writing process. Their belief was a constant source of motivation and inspiration. They sacrificed a lot of family time, so I could concentrate on the book.

I am also grateful to Hassan Shah and Faraz Zaidi, who engaged in countless intellectual debates with me. This enabled me to streamline my thinking and learn about varying topics of philosophy, politics and economy.

I would also like to thank Dr. Ismat Mirza and Madiha Furqan for their constant feedback and encouragement to make the book more concise and readable. Finally, I would like to thank my mother, who always encouraged me to seek knowledge.

PREFACE

Many great philosophers have talked about the concept of power. It has been a focal subject of many philosophical theories. It is a diabolical concept that has not only survived but also thrived in our societies. However, the development of power is shrouded in mystery. We also have very limited literature on what is the ideal model to construct power. There are primarily three power models which have gained prominence over the course of history. Perhaps, the first such model was given by Plato in the fourth century BCE when he conceptualized the idea of 'Philosopher King'. He believed that power should be given to a person based on their wisdom. They should oversee the creation of a just society through their knowledge. After him, came the idea of 'Prince' put forward by Niccolo Machiavelli in the sixteenth century CE. He believed that power should be exercised by a person who is pragmatic, a leader who is not afraid of using dubious and cunning methods to remain in power. In the nineteenth century CE, the third model came from Fredrich Nietzsche when he popularized the idea of 'Übermensch', a leader who is free from traditional frameworks and is bold enough to create their own standards. Apart from these three frameworks on power, we have works from Sun Tzu through 'Art of War' and Chankya through 'Arthashastra'. While Sun Tzu philosophy can be categorized as a combination of both Philosopher King and Prince, Chankya's work is dominantly Machiavellian in nature. We have hints of a fourth school of power model put forward by Stoic philosophers such as Epictetus and Seneca. They put forward the concept of 'Sage' who is an idealist and driven by inner peace. This model was further explored by Arthur Schopenhauer in the nineteenth century CE. However, their work was not directed as a standalone power model but as a way of life. Now, through this book, I am reopening the debate on Sage, perhaps the most underrated school on power. Through this book, I aim to refine the model proposed by Stoic philosophers and Schopenhauer and erect a parallel school of power which rivals Philosopher King, Prince and Übermensch. In Part I of this series on discussing power, I look upon the protagonist of the book, Sage, as they raise their stature in society and transform the society ruled by the antagonist of the book, a Machiavellian Prince.

Apart from proposing a fourth school of power, I investigate the psychological aspect of power. I try to answer why people vie for power. Why has it been the ultimate goal of many people across every race, religion, culture and sex? Added to this complex question is that we are yet to define power. We have examples of tyrants like Muammar Gaddafi, who used power to coerce people. But if power is coercion, how do we explain the influence of the pope? He exercises great power over a billion Catholics around the world, even when he forces no one to yield power to him. So, how do we define power?

There is a consensus that power is a measure of morality. We call Osama Bin Laden immoral as he masterminded the terrorist attacks on the world trade center while sitting in a position of power in Afghanistan, but if power is indeed a measure of morality, then why do not we call Nelson Mandela immoral when he went on a rampage to sabotage government properties in South Africa? Is power really a measure of morality?

Similarly, we are yet to know if power resides with the elite or if democracies have been able to dilute power to an ordinary person. India is the biggest democracy in the world, yet it had three prime ministers – Jawaharlal Nehru, Indira Gandhi and Rajiv Gandhi – coming from the same elite Nehru-Gandhi family. So, do only elites capture the position of power or do we have historical evidence of ordinary people emerging in society to thwart elitism. Is empowering a Sage a pipedream?

Many of these questions have been answered by some great philosophers whose works are cited in this book, but many others remain unanswered. This is mainly because the study of power spans an array of subjects. The desire for power is a subject in psychology, exercising power comes under sociology, the construction of power is studied under politics and the dynamics of power are studied in leadership. So, one must master all these subjects before answering all these questions. This book tries to combine philosophy, psychology, sociology and history in one place. It takes lessons from the lives of powerful people in history to develop a fourth model for constructing power. The book explains these concepts through the power of a Sage who rivals the power constructed by a Machiavellian Prince. The book is an antithesis to Niccolo Machiavelli. As you read through 21 chapters within these pages, you will understand the true complexity of power and how it operates in both the grand scheme of history and in the minute details of our everyday lives. The lessons learnt here will give you a deeper appreciation for the forces that shape our world and provide valuable insights for understanding and navigating today's power struggles.

INTRODUCTION

In Part I of the book, we sketch the genesis of power. We see that power is a tool which is not only about decision-making but also involves shaping opinions and dictating options. We look at different dimensions of power in Chapter 1. We then look at how power came into being in Chapter 2. We see that early humans exchanged their endless freedom and liberty to cater to their needs which paved way for power. In Chapter 3, we assess why power becomes an addiction to many. We see that those who vehemently seek their independence are those who vie for power as well. We then distinguish humanity into four groups in Chapter 4 based on their needs and independence. Here, we distinguish between the protagonist of the book, Sage, and the antagonist, Prince. In Chapter 5, we analyse that those who have needs and remain dependent on others keep yielding power.

In Part II of the book, we look at how power is harnessed. We open with Chapter 6, which discusses how needs of society evolve based on the environment they live in. In Chapter 7, we analyse how the institution of power changes with time and technology to cater to the evolving needs of society. In Chapter 8, we look at different sources of power based on physiological and psychological needs of society. We end the part with Chapter 9 by looking at the sources of power of Prince and Sage.

In Part III of the book, we look at different ways to exercise power. We start with Chapter 10, which mentions the pathways of power. These pathways have an embedded strategy, which is the topic of Chapter 11. The pathways and strategy pave the way for a game theory, which is discussed in Chapter 12.

In Part IV, we delve into a power struggle when a Sage emerges in the society. We first settle on how power is distributed in the society in Chapter 13. Based on that we develop a societal behaviour based on power distribution in Chapter 14. We then look at phases of society on how it moves based on societal behaviour in Chapter 15. At this point, we dwell on the life of a Sage and how it moves out of Slavery to challenge the Prince in Chapter 16. As the Sage starts its journey, it triggers a transition period in the society which may or may not be anarchic. This is discussed in Chapter 17. In Chapter 18, we look at the Sage's life goals as it aims to change the society.

In Part V of the book, we iron out the dividing line between a Sage and a Prince. In Chapter 19, we look at the standards of morality and ethics, which may be very subjective criteria to distinguish the Prince and Sage. In Chapter 20, we discuss possibilities on how Prince can be stopped from becoming an evil, while Chapter 21 talks about the personality traits of a Prince and how a Sage can be gauged by its action.

Part I

GENESIS OF POWER

Chapter 1

DEFINING POWER

Mastering others is strength. Mastering yourself is true power.

Lao Tzu

Cosimo de Medici was an Italian banker in fifteenth-century Florence. He took no part in democracy during the Italian Renaissance but enjoyed immense influence in political circles through his wealth. He was not a public representative but shaped the opinions of politicians from outside the parliament. He was arguably one of the most organized lobbyists in Europe. While Florentines looked upon politicians and autocrats for power, Medici intentionally stayed covert in his dealings and avoided direct power. This enabled him to stay relevant in politics even when things did not go well for some specific group of politicians. So, can we say that Medici had power? After all, he was not in a decision-making position. He was merely influencing politicians. So, is lobbying a sign of power? Or is power simply a phenomenon to control people and make decisions?

The English word 'power' is derived from the French word 'Pouvoir'. This in turn is derived from the Latin word 'Potentia', which means 'to be able'. Famous philosopher David Daiches Raphael defines power on similar lines.

The ability to make other people do what one wants them to do.

This is the most generic and widely understood definition of power, which focuses on the visible nature of power. It suggests that anyone who can control an action from taking place has power. This definition is also endorsed by Robert Dahl.

To explain this concept in detail, let us take an example of recreational drugs outlawed by legislators of a country. Police are enforcing this law by prosecuting violators. So, whoever is caught with recreational drugs is put behind bars. This acts as a deterrent to control the illegal action of smoking drugs. So, in this example, we can safely say that the police have power as they can control people from taking action. This definition of power is also similar to Karl Marx's definition of power, who believes that power resides with people who control resources. So, while Raphael and Dahl focused on the decision-making and control aspects of power, Marx focused on the economic aspects of power. He believes that humans require resources to live, and whoever controls the means of producing those resources wields power. He also believes those with economic power desire political power to strengthen their hand. In recreational drugs, though police control the actions they do not control the supply of drugs. Law passed by legislators prohibits the supply of drugs. So, according to Marx's definition of power, the power is with the legislative assembly, which legislates the means of production.

We may be tempted to say that power controls an action, but this definition fails to consider the desire to take an action. It does not give any heed to the psychological aspect of humans. It merely focuses on a single dimension of power – control and decision-making. However, power is a much more complex phenomenon than this definition suggests. If power is simply the ability to make people do things or control events, how would we explain a situation where someone shapes an opinion like Medici did? He had no action-controlling power. Would we say that opinion makers and lobbyists do not have power?

Max Weber plugged this obvious loophole in the definition of power. Weber defined the covert dimension of power. His definition of power focuses more on desires and opinions than actions taken and emphasizes the non-visible dimension of power. So, the vacuum left over by Dahl and Raphael was filled by Weber's definition of power. The best way to explain this is to look at the same example of recreational drugs. Though police are asking the masses not to consume recreational drugs, it is not the police whose desire is implemented. Police are merely implementing the law made by the legislators. However, it is possible that even the legislative assembly did not want to pass the directive to outlaw drugs; rather, they may have wanted to legalize drugs to earn revenue for the exchequer by taxing the consumption of drugs. But, perhaps, a lobby composed of affected families of drug abusers pressured the legislators to outlaw drugs. So, Weber would say that the lobby has power as it forced its opinion to outlaw drugs. The lobby materialized its desire over people's desire to consume drugs. While exercising this dimension of power, the public may be clueless about who has influenced the decision. That is why this dimension of power is covert in nature.

Another famous sociologist, Karl Deutsch, had a similar understanding of power as Weber. He opined that power is the ability to be in a conflict, resolve it and remove the obstacles. He looked at the power from the lens of a conflict rather than decision- making and shaping desires. In recreational drugs, while the legislative assembly is taking a decision, competing interest groups might be working in the background to get a decision in their favour. A lobby led by affected families of drug abusers directly conflicts with a lobby led by farmers who wanted to legalize drugs to make it a cash crop. While affected families are lobbying to ban drugs, farmers are lobbying to legalize the use of drugs. Since the legislators succumbed to the desire of affected families and decided to ban the drugs altogether, Deutsch would say that the lobby, composed of affected families, has power.

While Weber and Deutsch expanded our understanding of power, we may be tempted to say that overt and covert dimensions of power have completed the definition of power. However, we still have one situation which remains unanswered. Let us say that a pharmaceutical company comes up with the health benefits of recreational drugs in depression patients. But pharmaceutical companies fail to get any law passed by legislators for health purposes because of constant media scrutiny. Media has constantly been bombarding information against recreational drugs, even for medical purposes. They are citing several reasons, which is not allowing the limited use of drugs to be even on the agenda of the legislative assembly. Media, with their persistent narrative, has made drugs a taboo, so no legislator is willing to even debate the health benefits of drugs. Media in this situation is not forcing any decision but also not letting any debate in the legislative assembly. Here, the media wields power by subverting the agenda of the legislative assembly. This kind of power is unexplained in the earlier definitions of power. So, Peter Bachrach and Morton Baratz bridged this gap in the definition of power and highlighted the third dimension of power – agenda setting.

This type of power represents a situation where instead of decision-making, the power is preventing a decision from taking place by altering the agenda. This power represents non-decision-making rather than a decision-making process. This is usually done by eliminating options that run counter to one's interests. In the case of recreational drugs, while media is not pressurizing the legislators to ban drugs as a decision has been taken to outlaw drugs, the media is nudging the agenda by not allowing a debate to legalize drugs for depression patients. So, in this situation, the media will be assumed to have power over pharmaceutical companies trying to legalize limited drug use for depression patients. This type of power can be overt or covert and is usually the most underrated dimension of power.

Steven Lukes comprehends all the above dimensions of power by highlighting that power has three faces – decision- making, non-decision- making and shaping desires.

1. Decision-making: Any person or entity taking decisions or controlling actions has power. In this view, those who can demonstrate the physical nature of power will be perceived to have power.

2. Non-decision-making: This power is exercised by setting an agenda that does not counter one's interests. This can be done by offering options that give an illusion that the subject is taking a decision, but any option contrary to one's interest is already eliminated.
3. Shaping desires: This power wields neither from decision-making nor from non-decision making but by shaping desires in a group of people. These desires can be shaped directly or indirectly. Advertisements are usually considered a direct way to shape desires for products and services, while content marketing is a more subtle way to shape desires.

To look back at the power equation from an example of recreational drugs, the police have power as they can stop an action from taking place, and the legislative assembly has power as it is legislating on the ban of drugs. Both police and legislative assembly display the control and decision dimension of power. The interest group led by the affected families of drug abusers has power as they can lobby to outlaw drugs which runs counter to the interest group led by farmers. The emotional mother of a drug abuser has power as she can quell a desire to smoke drugs. All are displaying the opinion and desire dimension of power. Media has power as it can stop a decision from taking place. They are displaying the agenda-setting dimension of power. Although this example of recreational drugs may look simple, dissecting the problem reveals that our society is complex. Power is exercised by many members of society overtly and covertly at the same time. An individual's

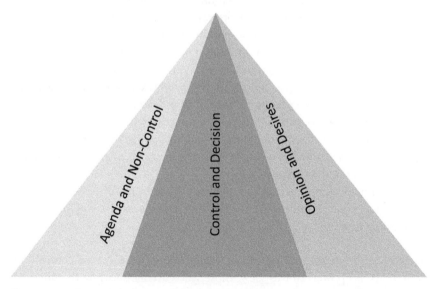

Figure 1.1 Three dimensions of power.

action of not smoking drugs reveals multiple layers of power depending on the underlying situation.

This example also reveals the lack of understanding by the public on who exercises power over them. They usually look at the decision-making or visible nature of power. They may feel that their local, state or federal government is in absolute power, paying no heed to the other two dimensions of power. They may protest or cry for help in front of the government when power may reside with some other entity. This dilemma was in full focus when we look at the Occupy Wall Street protests, where protesters were chanting slogans for a legitimate demand for economic justice. However, their anger was misdirected at Wall Street, a mere marketplace to trade securities. Since their demand was economic justice, they should have been lobbying or protesting in front of Capitol Hill. The correct way would have been to lobby politicians to pass legislation to increase taxes on the top 1 per cent wealthy individuals instead of trying to interrupt trade on Wall Street, where most account holders are common people, just like the protesters. By trying to interrupt trading activity, the protesters might harm more common people than the top 1 per cent individuals. The protesters will need to organize a lobby to compete against the lobby in Capitol Hill, not allowing taxes to be raised for the ultra-rich. Members of society should understand the power equation and appeal to those who may exercise power through different dimensions of power.

Another issue that comes to mind after looking at the Occupy Wall Street protests is that many people today possess power without recognizing it. They fail to understand that physical or visible power is not the only way to harness power. They may be completely oblivious to the influence embedded in them. They fail to recognize that they can influence actions, opinions and desires in one way or the other. In this sense, Medici's life should be understood as how he influenced and lobbied decision-makers in medieval Italy. This quality of recognizing power early sets powerful people apart from others. Those in power do not necessarily hold a top role in a societal hierarchy, but they influence behaviours in more than one way.

The founding father of Pakistan, Muhammad Ali Jinnah, was an example of a leader who could not recognize all three dimensions of power. He became inactive in India's politics after 1920 when his approach of constitutional struggle to gain self-rule was superseded by the non-violent *Satyagraha* boycott approach preached by Mohandas Gandhi. He was maligned in the political gathering, where a decision was made to adopt the Satyagraha movement. This event disillusioned him, and he left the Congress Party and bid adieu to political life. At that point, he was focusing on the visible dimensions of power. He became dispassionate when his approach to achieve autonomy was not endorsed by the Congress Party. However, he had gained power through

the opinion-making dimension of power where Eastern and Western popula-
tions of India had started believing in his way of gaining self-rule. He took
over a decade to understand the invisible power he had garnered. When he
returned to active politics, he continued his constitutional struggle and led the
independence of Pakistan.

To sum up, power is not only about decision making but it encompasses
other underrated dimensions as well. The society has to be wary on who controls the power structure and how it is being implemented.

Chapter 2

BIRTH OF POWER

Liberty may be endangered by the abuse of liberty, but also by the abuse of power.

James Madison

In sixteenth-century Europe, power was divided between church and the throne. The pope enjoyed tremendous influence over monarchs. His appreciation of the monarch was seen as a sign of legitimacy to the throne. So, when Martin Luther led the reformist agenda in Christianity, King Henry VIII jumped to defend the Catholic Church. Pope Leo X titled him 'Defender of the Faith' for his gusto defence which reinforced the House of Tudor. However, the king and the pope went on diverging paths when Henry VIII wanted a separation from his wife – Catherine of Aragon. She was the widow of Henry's elder brother Arthur. Henry married her in 1509, but they could not bear a male child. Henry's desire to have a male heir and marry Anne Boleyn led him to request the pope to annul his marriage. But new Pope Clement VII had taken the papacy. He categorically refused to annul the marriage as was the case with Catholic Church then. This led Henry towards creating a separate 'Church of England'. He persuaded the parliament to pass the 'Act of Supremacy', unifying the monarchy and the church. This watershed moment kickstarted the demolition of religious power across Europe. The unification of religious and political power within the monarch was complete. This incident raises a lot of questions, but a particular one is, why people deposited power in the pope and then King Henry VIII? What led to the birth of power in societies when it curbs individual freedom?

Humans were exposed to the concept of power from the onset. They saw power either at the time of their creation as propagated by creation mythologies or through observing the laws of the jungle as propagated by evolutionary theories. Whichever way we look, humans knew about power and its repercussions from day one. However, the institution of power could have died in its infancy. As is often the case, a concept is most vulnerable when it has not deeply rooted itself. Cannibalism was one such thing that could not root itself and died after the formation of agrarian societies. Similarly, slavery and fratricide greatly diminished as human societies evolved. However, power survived its initial days and became the basic building block in societies through a phenomenon called 'Social Contract'.

A social contract is a hypothesis that advocates that humans willingly or tacitly agree to stay together in a society. Humans are driven by their need to survive and self-preserve. So, in the initial days of humanity, our ancestors entered 'Pactus Unionis'. They agreed to come together to form a union to increase their chances of survival. Solitary living hampered humans' survival rate due to dangers posed by diseases, wild animals and the hostile environment around them. But communal living hedged these risks and greatly increased the survival rate. So, humans exchanged their unlimited freedom given by solitary living, where they could take any action with communal living, where some rules bounded their actions. These rules curbed unlimited freedom but protected the need to survive. The creation of these rules led to the institutionalization of power. The custodian of these rules became the first power holders. The social contract offered its subjects the option to either embrace communal living or go back into a solitary state where they could enjoy unlimited freedom in their actions. This is the same argument that Socrates used to justify his death penalty. He was rounded off by authorities and put behind bars for his views. He could escape prison with the help of his aides and live in exile or accept the death penalty. Socrates remained true to the social contract and accepted death by drinking poison. So, the concept of power, perceived as diabolical in the modern age, as it curbs freedom, was strengthened and institutionalized by none other than our ancestors. They preferred their need for self-preservation over freedom, leading to the survival of power in our societies. They willingly gave away their independence by submitting to power where they could ensure their life.

The concept of a social contract is often critiqued for not complying with historical evidence. The anthropological records prove that humanity started by living in society rather than in solitude. On the other hand, social contract advocates that the human race started its journey from solitary living. Although this criticism invalidates the social contract timeline, it still does not explain the rationale behind communal living. The first humans still faced the same dilemma while living in a society. They either had to embrace the rules of society or defect to a place where they could live a lonely life with no rules. So, one may disagree with the chronology of the social contract, but there are thin grounds to dispel the arguments on how a social contract institutionalizes power.

All social contractarian philosophers agree that humanity's sole purpose of entering a social contract was to seek protection in exchange for freedom. But they disagree on the level of freedom compromised in a social contract.

Based on that, all contractarian philosophers can be distinguished into three types of social contract – singular, distributive and pluralistic. Singular social contract is when laws curb the highest levels of freedom as laws are made and driven by one powerful institute. Distributive social contract is when members of society agree together to curtail as much amount of freedom as deemed necessary to warrant survival, while pluralistic social contract is when people decide their own rules, which curb minimal levels of freedom. Let us look at some famous social contract theories based on the level of freedom they advocate.

Singular Social Contract

Thomas Hobbes believes that social contract was a necessity in early societies. The main virtues of humans were force and fraud. They accumulated power and did not back down from trampling on others' rights. They did not display any empathy which led to poor rates of survival. Hence, people desired some rules to protect their rights. They agreed to curtail their freedom to empower a strong entity that could make and enforce rules. These rules were to protect human lives and punish the violators. All members of society followed the same set of rules made by one singular power. This meant that everyone's freedom was equally curtailed. Hobbes strongly believes in an authoritative and empowered entity to make these rules, as human nature cannot be trusted with any freedom. He believes in the maximum curtailment of individual freedom.

Hans Morgenthau is another philosopher who was not a social contractarian but a classical realist. However, his realist theory is based on the same lines as the Hobbesian social contract. He believes that nations reflect the basic human instinct of survival where they prefer their own interest. Their national priorities take precedence over any other moral principle. This necessitates realism and accumulation of power. Morgenthau believes that to stop this accumulation of power by individual nations, it is imperative to create a mechanism to balance power among sovereign states. World peace is impossible until the world community comes together to shun their national interests to strengthen a power, which would foster world peace. In Morgenthau's social contract of nations, individual countries, much like individuals, must let go of their interests and freedom to create a mechanism to establish peace.

Distributive Social Contract

Jean-Jacques Rousseau believes that the general will of society makes rules. General will is a collection of everyone's rights where no one is under- or over-represented, much like a functioning democracy. Since the general will does not represent an individual's will, the freedom of the individual is curtailed only by the general will. The power ensures that the remaining rights of people are protected by complying with the same rules of the general will. So, when an individual violates these rules, they violate a part of their own will. Rousseau believes that the general will acts as insurance against mutiny as no one likes to violate their own rights.

Another great philosopher, Immanuel Kant, also believes in this type of social contract. He believes a social contract is a natural conclusion to the 'Categorical Imperative'. It is a moral law of reciprocity where people act in a way which they believe others should act. He emphasizes that humans may act according to their natural self. He puts a lot of emphasis on individual freedom but limits the boundaries of freedom by the universal law of reciprocity. Kant believes that morality is the core reason people shun the state of nature and come together in a society. They agree to bow down to a power so that everyone lives under the same laws of morality. The role of power is, thus, to ensure that people may live in a society if they remain within the spheres of morality. In Kant's social contract, individual freedom is curtailed to the extent of morality.

John Rawls expanded on Kant's social contract. He developed a thought experiment of 'Original Position', whereby people are asked to make rules of a hypothetical society behind a 'Veil of Ignorance'. The veil makes people unaware of what social status or gender they will have in the society they will be a part of. He believes that provided no information is available to them about their own status, people will make laws that appeal to justice, morality and impartiality. They will not make rules that may benefit or harm any segment of society as they may end up as victims of their own rules. Thus, Rawls's social contract curtails people's freedom to the extent of empowering an institute that not only implements laws of morality but also includes elements of impartiality and justice.

Pluralistic Social Contract

John Locke believes that it is everyone's responsibility to protect natural rights. Natural rights are God-given, so those who trample upon these rights deserve punishment. However, there is no precedent on the quantum of punishment. The punishments may be arbitrary if left to individuals. Hence, the members of society must institutionalize power to be a judge between people in disputes and to award punishments to the violators of natural rights. This will ensure that not only are people's rights protected but also violators are punished according to the same precedents. Locke's social contract appeals to judicial power as he believes that people are free in their actions while power has a limited scope of awarding punishment to violators of natural rights.

Pierre-Joseph Proudhon is a libertarian and founder of the anarchic school of thought. His social contract is radical in approach as he is the first to mix the elements of socialism with liberalism. He is a fierce critic of Rousseau as he believes people do not voluntarily compromise on their freedom. Instead, he believes that people make their own social contract rules. Proudhon emphasizes individual's liberty and strongly disagrees with external stimuli to make rules. He believes that a social contract arises from commerce between people. The transactions between people are governed by certain rules developed and implemented by people themselves. These transactions form the backbone of a social contract. In Proudhon's social contract, people curtail their freedom based on their interactions with other people.

The different versions of the social contract show that freedom and security are inversely linked. The more security one wants, the more freedom they must give up. Humans have to opt if they want freedom or security. The institution of power is, thus, to make rules of engagement or simply put, a social contract depending upon the level of freedom people give up. The responsibility of power is, nonetheless, to ensure security and protection. The social contract determines the level of security and freedom in any society. The more freedom people require, the less security they get back and less power they yield and vice versa. There are pros and cons to each social contract, but each social contract has been witnessed in our society, where a singular, distributive and pluralistic approach has been adopted to ensure human preservation.

The current regimes in the Gulf region display a singular social contract where the highest level of individual freedom is curtailed. A strong central body holds power that makes and governs the rules of engagement. Western democracies display a distributive social contract, where the general will of people curtails individual freedom. They elect their representatives who make rules of engagement. On the other hand, countries like Switzerland, New Zealand and Denmark display a pluralistic social contract, where people curtail their individual freedom minimally. They participate in referendums to decide the principles of freedom and security. When we look at history, we see a general trend that each social contract starts from a singular social contract and progresses towards a pluralistic social contract. Rarely does a society start from a pluralistic social contract. The positioning of a social contract determines the levels of freedom and progression of a society.

When we look at King Henry VIII from the lens of a social contract, his individual freedom to marry and choose his partner was curtailed by the pope. Only the pope could adjudicate on second marriage. Though it was not

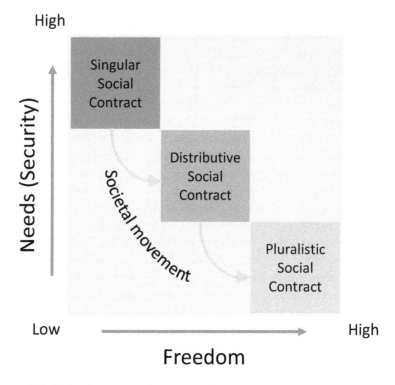

Figure 2.1 Societal movement based on social contract.

only Henry but the whole Catholic Europe had also entered a social contract with the Vatican. The religious authority was held singularly by The Holy See. In exchange for bowing down to the institution of the Vatican, the pope blessed the throne, which imparted political security to the kingdom. So, when Henry wanted to exercise his personal freedom to marry, he had to either break his relation with the Vatican and risk political uncertainty or continue to abide by the rules set out by the pope. He decided in the former and invented his own social contract governed by the Church of England. This created a heightened singular social contract in England, where Henry held both political and religious power. This event had unintended consequences, whose ripples were felt over a century, culminating in the English Civil War.

It is pertinent to mention here that there is a general misunderstanding in modern societies that freedom is a fundamental right, when the reality is that most people believe that it is life that is the most basic right. Freedom comes after the survival of life is ensured. This is also advocated in Maslow's hierarchy of needs. Freedom can satisfy ego and psychological needs, but it cannot ensure a physiological need to secure life. Our ancestors have bartered a part of our personal freedom for personal security. Humans agreed to the norms of social contact, whereby we culminated our freedom in favour of living harmoniously in a society. We accepted that the option remains open for us to return to the solitary state of nature or bow down to the powers held by the social contract. The whole purpose of a social contract is to develop an uneasy alliance between the members of society so peace can be ensured. However, if someone is trying to expand the boundaries of their freedom beyond what a social contract warrants, they may be unknowingly breaking it. A theoretical scenario exists where humans may attain unlimited freedom, but that may come at the expense of personal protection. The movie *Purge* highlights this hypothetical state where people have unlimited freedom for a night which results in revenge killings. We also witnessed similar mayhem unleashed in parts of Africa, Sudan, Libya and Syria. The revolutionary movements in those countries tried to expand the limits of freedom warranted by their singular social contract. These movements tried to pursue freedom beyond what their social contract entitled them to. It resulted in voiding the social contract and plunged the whole region into chaos. There are no laws in these countries that give people unlimited freedom. People in these countries are now free to roam, eat and enjoy lawlessness, but they are also free to fight, plunder and rape. The result is a mass exodus in the form of refugees from these regions as many do not want to jeopardize their life. These refugees have landed in various parts of Europe and willingly entered another social contract prevalent in their adopted countries. However, they stuck to the same principle of exchanging freedom with security. The refugees prioritized their personal security over living a life without rules. Though we see this happening currently in Africa, Sudan, Libya and Syria, humans worldwide have faced the same dilemma of trading freedom with security in every era.

The current rights movement for freedom of speech and expression may have also missed the same logic that the boundaries of freedom are not limitless. Communities in every part of the world have entered varying sets of social contracts depending on the region's cultural, religious, historical and political sensitivities. The varying nature of these social contracts may or may not allow endless freedom unless the social contract is broken. Once the social contract is trespassed, there may be unintended consequences such as the anarchy prevailing in Middle East. So, one must know the ground realities of the social contract prevalent in the region before expanding the horizons of freedom.

Chapter 3

WHY IS POWER AN ADDICTION?

Power is the ultimate aphrodisiac.

Henry Kissinger

Benedict Arnold was a famous military general who fought in the US War of Independence. His success in the Continental Army started after he captured Fort Ticonderoga. He consequently led many battlefields with valour and suffered combat injuries too. However, after five years of fighting against British troops and bypassed for promotions, he switched sides and defected to his former enemy, where he was put in charge of fighting against his former colleagues. Though he gained a position of power, his betrayal led to his name becoming synonymous with treason. When we look around history, Arnold is not the first to pursue the betrayal path. Many before and after him took similar trajectories to grab power. So, what led Arnold to take such an extraordinary step? Why do people take such outrageous decisions to gain power?

To understand why people like power, we first must understand the concept of 'freewill'. Freewill is a unique phenomenon that gives humans a sense of freedom. It helps us to freely determine what to eat, what to wear and where to go. We are humans because of our freewill. We are differentiated from machines because we can make independent choices induced by the freewill. Freewill is independent in the sense that it is not tangible. It cannot be caged. No one can govern freewill. Our ambitions are tied to our freewill, which forces us to take extraordinary ventures. The human progression from a cave(wo)man to a space(wo)man has been made possible because of our freewill. Our ancestors' freewill to have better food and secure shelter propelled us to develop the complex world we live in today.

It is a pity that little research is available on freewill. Humans have mastered many areas of science, but we have yet to determine what triggers freewill. Some technology and social media companies have been able to nudge freewill, but they are far from controlling or measuring it. We have invented physics to predict the future when the outcome is not dependent on human decisions, but we have to use probabilities when humans are part of decision-making. It is mainly because physics is governed by universal laws, which gives us certainty, but freewill is not governed by any laws, which gives us an uncertain future. That is why we have to make use of probability. As long as human actions remain governed by freewill, we will never be able to determine the future course of actions.

Many believe that time machines will be the biggest breakthrough in human development. It is because it will help us to know the future course of actions. However, the key to the future lies in understanding freewill rather than trying to develop a time machine. The day we know how freewill works, we can decode the genesis of human actions. This will unlock the future as human actions become predictable. We will then not require a time machine but decode freewill to help us navigate the future. The probability will become a redundant subject once freewill becomes predetermined. Until that happens, freewill remains a great variable that will keep changing history while being confined in a small space in the human skull.

A side question arises from people who believe in the 'deterministic' school of thought that freewill is a hoax and everything is predestined. They believe that actions we take directly result from prior actions or fate. They believe that freewill is an invention of humans to give them an illusion of freedom. However, the deterministic school has limitations because if everything is deterministic, then someone should be able to determine the future as well. Since all the outcomes are an effect of past events or fate, the future can also then be determined with some certainty. But the reality is humans are not even close to knowing the future. However, we are heading towards an artificial intelligence–backed era where the future may become deterministic. Powerful artificial intelligence algorithms may be able to decide human actions. These algorithms will be based on the previous life events of an individual. They will enable us to predict future human actions. These algorithms will help to eliminate aberrations in human decision-making. Prior actions and data points in the life of humans will indeed become a key to predict the future. However, the rise of such artificial intelligence–backed algorithms is far. First, the technology is still under development, and then it will be subject to political, cultural and social approval. Also, whenever artificial intelligence takes over, it will still be incapable of governing humans in unchartered territory. It can be a good judge when a precedent is there, but it cannot help us when variables are unknown. So, keeping this in mind, the deterministic school fails to answer many crucial questions to thwart the freewill school. However, if we believe in the deterministic school for argument's sake, we must look at an equivalent word of freewill in the deterministic dictionary. Since the deterministic school believes prior actions or fate are the driver for future actions while free-will school believes that freewill is the instigator of future actions, then freewill becomes equivalent to prior events and fate. So freewill can be read in conjunction with prior actions or fate when reconciling freewill and deterministic schools of thought.

Now that we have established what is freewill and determinism, let us look at how they pave the way for desires. Freewill or prior life events trigger desires in an individual. For instance, the desire to have a big house can be due to an individual's free thinking to have a luxurious life or induced due to the upbringing in a small house. This desire may remain confined within the mind without triggering any action. It remains harmless and remains controlled. However, if this desire triggers an action, it progresses towards becoming a need. A need is an action induced by a desire. This need can be physiological or psychological. In the above example, if owning a big house did not induce any action, it remains a desire. However, if someone starts working towards materializing the desire by working in a highly paid job to get a mortgage, then the desire to buy a big house has become a need. Many believe that 'desires' and 'needs' are interchangeable words depending on the level of necessity. If owning something is a necessity of life, then it is a need; if it is not, then it is a desire. However, this is a subjective view of segregating desires from needs. Each person operates at a different level of necessity. So, this distinction becomes subjective. That is why the best way to differentiate between the two is to identify if an action has been taken. When desire leaves the metaphysical realm and enters the physical realm through an action, it becomes a need. Multiple philosophical views postulate the purpose behind taking an action. These views range from judging the action from the greater-good lens as explained in utilitarianism, to the individual-good perspective as preached by hedonism. Irrespective of the philosophical views, needs force an action and the action can be taken when someone has power. Hence, an action is the result of a need while need is the root cause of power. Power came into being as soon as needs were created in human development. The scramble for power is the side-effect of needs.

To elaborate on this, let us take an example of a simple act of eating an apple. The desire to eat an apple can be due to its shine or feeling hungry. If the desire is not triggering any action, nothing happens. It remains a desire. We can keep on thinking of eating an apple without any hassle. However, if we take an action to materialize our desire, then it becomes a need. If the ownership of the apple is not contested, then no power is required. But let us say there is another person who also desires to eat the same apple. In this situation, the action of eating the apple will be decided by who can invoke more power. A physical duel or some other mechanism will decide the ownership of the apple. Whoever has more power gets to eat it. Hence, to fulfil the need, one must take an action and to take an action, power is garnered. Power, thus, becomes an enabler to fulfil the need. The more power one has, the higher the chances of fulfilling the need. The liking for power is not driven by any sinister purpose, as perpetrated by many intellectuals, but by the innocent desire to fulfil a need. It is a separate debate though, if the underlying need itself is evil or virtuous.

This analogy of explaining power through the lens of owning an apple can be well understood by studying the Abrahamic mythology of expelling Adam and Eve from the heavens. The original sin of the first humans was the desire to eat the fruit from the forbidden tree. But God commanded humans not to have any fruit from that tree. When Adam materialized his desire through an action, he crossed his desire realm. He contested the territory of God. He portrayed himself as more powerful, which did not go well with the Deity. He was punished and banished to Earth.

To explain the correlation between power and needs further, let us assume that we are walking alone on a dark street. A beggar is lurking around the corner. He is short of cash and hopes to get it from us. Nothing happens if he keeps thinking of having our cash and does not intend to materialize his desire. He can keep on thinking, and we can walk past him. But if he takes an action, his desire is converted into a need. His need is pitted against our need. Let us assume that we do not intend to give the beggar any cash. So, there is a clash where one wants cash, and the other does not want to give anything away. The beggar decides to beg, but since our need is not to give any cash, we refuse to budge to his pleading. The beggar is unsuccessful in implementing his need. But we successfully implement our need, as we can say no to the beggar. We have more power than the beggar to fulfil the need. But if the same beggar becomes a mugger by buying a gun. He forces us to give him cash through the power of the gun. In this situation, his chance of fulfilling the need goes higher. Notice when the beggar has no power, he cannot get his need, but as soon as he demonstrates his power through the gun, he can fulfil his need. In both instances, neither the beggar nor our need changes, but the materialization of need is done by the entity with more power. In the first instance, we quenched the need due to the power differential, and in the second, the mugger implemented his need due to the power he garnered through the gun.

When we dissect the story of Benedict Arnold, we see a similar maxim. He wanted to dictate the matters of war while his superiors ignored him. He was sidelined by his generals and superseded by his juniors. He could not materialize his need. This forced him to choose the path of treason. He defected to the opposition camp, which allowed him to grasp power. The added power quotient allowed him to dictate war tactics. He fulfilled his need through harnessing new power.

When we dissect the chronology of power, freewill triggers a desire in the human mind. Desires pave the way for harnessing power. Once enough power is garnered, action is taken to convert a desire into a need. Need is fulfilled by the entity that garners more power. The more power one has, the more chances of realizing a need. Hence, power is a mere tool for the physical manifestation of a desire.

If we expand the above example at a broader level, we will know why power is an aphrodisiac. At any given time, humans can either jail their desire or garner power to fulfil their need. If they jail their desire, then it leads to depression, but if they exhibit their desire, then they must garner power which leads to clashes. When we look closely, we see that it is not power that leads to clashes but desires which is the root cause of these clashes. These desires are governed by freewill. Thus, lust for power will continue, and people will keep battling until freewill remains. For power to die, freewill must die alongside it.

It is also pertinent to mention that many libertarians have confused power with the human desire to subjugate others. They believe that power is a mere tool to oppress people. Libertarians believe that power is an invention of tyrants to curb freedom. But the reality is that power is in existence because people have needs. They pursue power to have the liberty to take any action. Libertarians also demand liberty due to their freewill. Freewill forces an individual to become independent in their actions. Hence, libertarians' views are driven from the narrow angle of freedom alone, ignoring that power is the unintended consequence of freewill. No one can claim to be independent without having the requisite power. Power is the connection between freewill and independence.

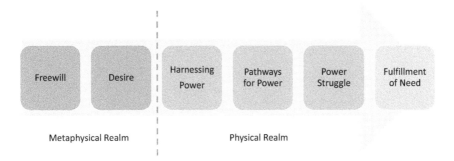

Figure 3.1 Conversion of desire into action.

If we look back at the story of Adam, we see this connection clearly. Adam was commanded by God not to eat the apple. He did not have liberty in his actions because he did not have the power to do so. God had much superior power. So, when Adam ate that apple, he trespassed his bounds of liberty. This did not go well with God, and he was banished from the heavens. This shows that independence can only be exercised by those who have the power to do so.

Chapter 4

WHO PURSUES POWER?

Power is given only to those who dare to lower themselves and pick it up. Only one thing matters, one thing; to be able to dare!

Fyodor Dostoevsky

Before Martin Luther King Jr became a symbol of the civil rights movement in the United States in twentieth century, Rosa Parks started the resistance against racial discrimination. She proclaimed power by instigating the 'Montgomery Bus Boycott'. She was an African American working-class lady. On 1 December 1955, she was riding a bus when she was told by the bus driver – James Blake – to make way for white passengers. The 'Jim Crow' laws of that era authorized the segregation of passengers based on ethnicity, but that day Parks defied those laws. She took a stand against racial discrimination. She was taken off the bus, humiliated and fined for obstructing the law, but she could have been lynched as well, like Emmett Till. Till was another African American lynched merely three months earlier on racial grounds. However, Parks stood tall and gathered all power to defy the racist status quo. So, what led her to endanger her life and take a stand? Can we develop a model to predict the most likely candidates to pursue power?

We have already established in the previous chapter that people require power to materialize their needs. These needs range from basic ones to complex ones. Survival is the most basic human need, and humans like to preserve their life at all costs. They resist any action which threatens their life. Humans are born with this trait which ensures the continuity of the human race. Most philosophers who have written extensively on human nature agree that preserving life is the most basic human ingredient. While the protection of life is a critical human need, there are many other needs as well. The strategy to fulfil those needs is driven by the resources one has at their disposal. If they can independently fulfil those needs without any help from others, then it is presumed that they have power to do so. However, they yield power if they depend on others to fulfil their needs. The decision to remain independent or dependent while fulfilling a need determines if the person is a contender to pursue power.

To explain this concept further, let us re-examine the actions of the mugger and the beggar from the previous chapter. When the mugger points a gun at us to swindle our wallet, he has chosen independence to ensure that he is not relying on us to give him cash willingly. Before robbing, he pursued power through the gun to make his need independent, where he was sure he would get money. Contrast this to the actions of a beggar. He is choosing to beg for money rather than snatch it from pedestrians. He is allowing the subjectivity of pedestrians to fulfil his need. He remained dependent on fulfilling his need. Notice that the needs of both the mugger and the beggar are to get money from others, but their actions display distinct levels of freedom. Without a gun, the mugger is also a beggar, but the mugger chooses to control the resources to fulfil his need while the beggar chooses not to. The mugger chooses threat to siphon money, while the beggar chooses to plead. So, the same need displays two distinct levels of freedom. Likewise, everyone has a choice if they choose independence or dependence to fulfil their needs. Hence, power is a tricky game where each type of need requires a different level of freedom.

Keeping the actions of the mugger and the beggar in mind, we can plot four distinct types of people on the need vs. freedom matrix. Since survival forms the bottommost part of the need hierarchy, the distinction of humanity can be better judged by looking at survival need than any other arbitrary need. We will notice that the need for survival induces a different level of freedom. Based on this, we can divide humanity into four categories in the following 'Power Matrix'.

The first iteration of people who like to vie for power are those with a high sense of maintaining their freedom even if it comes at the expense of survival. They are 'Sages' in their conduct. They are possessed by their ideology and beliefs which force them to remain fiercely independent. They display suicidal tendencies in their actions. These people are oddballs who pursue independence without worrying about their life. They short-circuit their survival needs and pursue their independence vehemently to implement their ideology. The extreme actions to maintain their freedom symbolize their competitive tendencies. The world usually remembers these kinds of people as freedom fighters or terrorists, depending on the perspective used to gauge their actions. But, irrespective of being tagged as a hero or a villain in society, they are driven by what they believe in than what they are up against.

Tipu Sultan enjoys legendary status in South Asia for his bravery. He led a spirited charge against the advancing East India Company even though he knew he was outpowered. His intention to keep English occupiers at bay

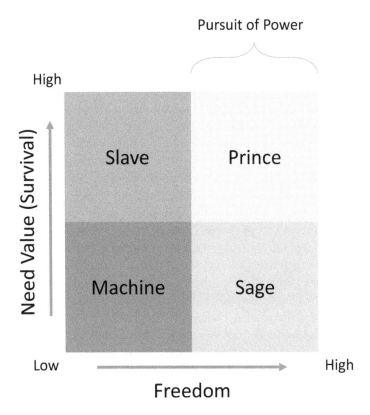

Figure 4.1 Power matrix of humanity.

pinned him against a much superior army. He fought valiantly on the battlefield, only to be killed. He did not care about his need to survive while pursuing his independence. Rosa Parks also falls in this category of people who pursued her freedom over survival. White supremacists could have lynched her when she defied race laws. The ordeal of Till could have stopped her from taking a stand, but she overcame her survival bias. She pursued independence in her views and stood against racial discrimination.

Avshalom Haviv is an example of a Sage terrorist. He was part of the Zionist outfit Irgun. He fought against the British mandate of Palestine, where he put up a spirited fight to break Acre prison and rescue other jailed insurgents. In the ensuing combat, he was captured by British troops and later hanged. Had he prioritized his survival instinct, he would not have taken the suicidal mission to rescue his comrades. Similarly, corporate whistle-blowers fall into this category as they commit symbolic suicide to execute what they believe in. Antoine Deltour defaced tax avoidance schemes where he prioritized his independence of principles over saving his corporate career. Many corporate activists, such as Tim Bray, also fall into this category. These activists and whistle-blowers criticize corporate policies only to endanger their own corporate careers.

A few tyrants may also seep into Sage category if the criteria are only ideology and independence. Adolf Hitler is one such controversial example driven by his freedom and ideology than his survival instinct. His life as a soldier in World War 1 points us in that direction where he fought valiantly for the German cause. Post World War 1, his first attempt to take down the government in 1923 also gives us a similar hint. He was driven by his ideology to implement ultra-German nationalism. But since he did not have enough power then, he could not topple the incumbent power structure. He was charged with treason and put behind bars. It took him almost a decade after the events of 'Beer Hall Putsch' to become powerful enough to dethrone the government. He then became a fascist dictator who implemented his model of ultra-German nationalism until he met his end by committing suicide. Had he not been a Sage, he would have decided to live behind bars and compromise on his independence. Though he does qualify the criteria of a Sage based on ideology and independence, he does not qualify the criteria laid out in Chapter 21. So, for the purpose of clarity, Hitler is not regarded as a Sage in this book.

To sum up, Sages do not care about their survival or what they are up against. They are uni-focused on their ideology, beliefs and thoughts driven by their freedom. These people never embrace pragmatism. When implementing their freedom, they may even get killed. This breed is an incredibly special category of people, as they are the bravest yet most dangerous and unpredictable among humanity. They shake up the entire power structure but they are remembered in history not for claiming the throne but for their beliefs and freedom. This category of people is reserved for heroes on one end and terrorists on the other.

The second iteration of people who vie for power are those with a high sense of implementing their freedom coupled with a high trait of survivability. Machiavellian 'Princes' are defined by both their freedom and survival instinct. They control the dynamics of the ecosystem they live in. They become incumbents in holding the power structure together. They like to ensure that things get done based on their desire without endangering their self-preservation. Most of the people in this category display pragmatism than ideology. Hence, they only wage a battle when they are sure they can succeed. That is why they are more likely to become Prince of the system than dying trying to topple the incumbent power structure. Unlike the Sage group, they garner enough power before attempting a coup. Their decision to wage a battle is triggered by their chances to survive, but Sages' decisions to wage a battle are driven by their beliefs and principles.

The unique combination of freedom and survival instinct prevailing in thePrince also explains why many fascists and dictators like to cling to power. They continue to hold Prince status by purging people who challenge their freedom. They continue to fulfil their needs by holding the pivotal status in society. However, when pressure mounts on them, they use power to ensure their survival instead of retiring. They foresee that they may be purged much like they did their challengers. So, they cling to power till the very end. They gather as much power as necessary to ensure their life. Hence, the best way to non-violently overthrow a Prince is by assuring them that their survival is guaranteed. That way, Prince is pushed into the slave category where their life is ensured.

Saddam Hussein is a good example to explain this iteration of people. He proclaimed power after the 'Baath Party Purge' events in 1979. He waited for 11 years as a deputy to Ahmed Hassan Al-Bakr. When he realized that he had the support of enough officials, he waged a coup against his party leader and officials. This is the evidence that he was not driven by an ideology but by his survival. He waged a coup when he knew he would succeed. He waited for over a decade for his moment to seize the throne. Saddam then purged all his opposing candidates to ensure that there was no countercoup. Later, when the US-led coalition toppled him, he ran for his life and hid in caves rather than waging a battle. This tells us that Saddam was a pragmatist rather than an ideologist. His survival instinct first forced him to wait for 11 years to topple the incumbent and then assassinate anyone who could challenge him. Later, when he could not resist the onslaught of the US invasion, he hid himself in caves to ensure his survival.

Notice the difference between the lives of Tipu and Saddam. One was a Sage, and other a Prince. Both sat on the throne and were fighting against a formidable army. Tipu was up against the East India Company, and Saddam was up against US troops. Both knew their survival was in danger, but Tipu fought and died like an ideologist on the battlefield while Saddam ran and hid like a pragmatist to save his life. This stark difference highlights the difference between a Sage and a Prince. A Sage and a Prince may both control the power structure, but a Sage displays freedom and ideology when threatened, while a Prince displays survival and pragmatism when challenged.

Among Prince, several people exist who temporarily lower their survival instinct without worrying if they can win. They display Sage tendencies in their behaviour until they can displace the incumbent. Aung San Suu Kyi qualifies in this set of people. She was on a self-imposed exile after Ne Win imposed martial law in 1962. She prioritized survival when Myanmar plunged into dictatorship. She stayed away from politics to ensure her life. However, after the '8888 uprising', Suu Kyi had garnered enough power to wrestle the military junta. The public was behind her to wage a battle. So, she returned in 1988 and won the 1990 elections only to be house arrested. However, this time she did not resort to escaping Myanmar. She did not choose exile even when the opportunity came to take care of her ailing husband. Instead, she fought the military might while confined to a house arrest. After 1990, she developed Sage tendencies driven by her democratic ideology. She peacefully confronted the dictatorship until she returned to power after the 2015 elections. However, she resorted back to showing survivor bias after proclaiming power. She blinded herself to Rohingya atrocities and allowed the military-led massacre in North Myanmar. The Sage tendency would have warranted her to pin herself against the junta, but instead, she kept quiet until she was deposed. Her life post-2015 is defined by survival, while the period between 1990 and 2015 is defined by an ideology.

Thus, the Prince group will be composed of people who show valour to implement their freedom but also extreme selfishness to survive. They never get the same accolades as a Sage group who display selflessness against all odds. This class of people comprises fascists on one end and controversial leaders on the other.

The third group of people are 'Slaves'. The concept does not mean medieval slavery but those who willingly let go of their independence in favour of their needs. This is where most of the human population resides. This group has a high sense of survival but is too scared to foray into displaying their freedom. They are driven by their preservation and do not adopt the Prince or Sage trajectory to exhibit their freedom. They do not believe in contesting the power game and instead resort to confining themselves to living a suppressed life. This group easily concedes power whenever they are pitted against someone. Like other humans, they possess freedom tendencies. They also think freely but do not materialize their freedom because they lack the internal motivation to become independent. In a few cases, Slaves do not exhibit freedom even in their thoughts. They are burdened by the Prince's beliefs and biases, which drive them. They shun or block their free thinking altogether. Their freedom and thoughts are compromised in those cases. Princes hammer them with ideas on theology, economic system and politics. Slaves willingly or tacitly subjugate their freedom to the beliefs perpetrated by Princes. They are groomed to identify with a specific clique. Slaves are easy victims of social influence. Social influence is of three types, as postulated by Herbert Kelman. (1) Compliance – The influence over a person to comply with an opinion or situation even when the person disagrees with it; for example, several South Africans complied with apartheid even when they disagreed with it. (2) Identification – The influence to like or follow someone because the whole society likes or adopts it, for example, several South Africans identified themselves as white even though they did not believe in any racial supremacy. (3) Internalization – The influence to adopt and agree to a norm, belief or tradition; for example, many White South Africans resorted to supporting the white government policies as it benefitted them.

A side question arises here: all humans carry some beliefs and biases, so everyone falls into the Slave category. The answer is we become a Slave as we are carrying someone's ideas while subjugating our free thoughts. If we free ourselves from all kinds of beliefs and biases and develop our thinking from scratch, we can fight back our freedom and thoughts. That way. we become Sages. However, if someone else has indoctrinated or hammered opinions on us with no critical thinking by ourselves, then we yield power to a Prince and degrade ourselves to Slavery.

The main characteristic of Slaves is that they fear others and lack the mettle to materialize their freedom. They live under immense pressure and succumb to all types of power. The mugger is successful in taking the wallet of these kinds of people as they cannot retaliate. Fascist regimes take hold in these cultures where no one dares to display their freedom. This group confines itself within the narrow aisle of survival, where they keep on yielding power to others who push them to the corner. The Slave category forms the bulk of humanity. These people are minions who walk the planet but leave behind no legacy. They are neither remembered nor recalled on any page of history because of their selfish yet natural desire to survive. The only way these people break the shackles of slavery is by learning the art of retaliation. If they retaliate, they display freedom by becoming a Sage.

The fourth iteration in the power matrix is comprised of 'Machines'. This group is defined by having neither freedom nor survival instinct. This group can be crushed without fear of retaliation, which demonstrates their zero-survival instinct and can be ordered to work relentlessly, which demonstrates their lack of freedom. While Machines form the lowest level in the power matrix, they form the epitome of loyalty. The extreme form of loyalty can be expected only from this group as they display no freedom or survival bias. This group acts like mechanical machines. Just like a real-life machine keeps churning until it breaks down or executes the task until the operator powers it off. Similarly, this group demonstrates traits that highlight its non-existent survival and freedom instinct. However, any change in the composition of the Machine's survival or freedom is a doomsday scenario for the Prince. If Machines' survival instinct goes up, then they become unpredictable. They may stop midway during the execution of an instruction if their survival is endangered. If their freedom goes up, then they may stop taking commandments at all. They may display their own thoughts and display independence in their behaviour. So, either way, any fiddling with the composition of freedom or survival of Machines is apocalyptic for the Prince.

While we may like to believe that in the construction of society, no human resides in the Machine group as every human has at least some levels of freedom and survival but few people who are mentally or socially challenged show traits of Machines. They are neither fussed by the dangers around them nor bothered about forcing an action. Many teenage suicide bombers display traits of Machines. They are brainwashed to act in a way their Prince has told them to act, and they are not fussed by their survival as they are aware that they will die because of their suicide attack. Crafting a Machine out of a human is one of the most difficult tasks ever undertaken by a Prince. If people in the Machine group start showcasing their freedom or survival, they usually take the trajectory of the Prince. The results of their actions are occasionally very disturbing. This is the subject of many fictional sociopaths and anti-heroes who suddenly start showcasing their freedom and survival. In the corporate world, many CEOs also display this trajectory from displaying asocial tendencies to controlling corporate empires.

Barring the aberrations in Machine traits, the world will become utopian the day there exists only people belonging to the Machine and Prince groups. Prince will use their power to exercise their freedom of actions on people residing in Machines, while machines will show predictable behaviour in executing the instructions of Prince. There will be no friction in the social order. Society will display exemplary functional behaviour. However, this is far from a real-life scenario as it is impossible to construct a society composed of only Princes and Machines. All societies have a Prince, a few Sages and plenty of Slaves with near-zero Machines. Most of the deviation in the world order is driven by people residing in the Sage group. It will remain humans' biggest tragedy that the most erratic and brave people belonging to the Sage group are the biggest drivers of disruption in society. Their ideology to challenge the Prince remains the biggest source of clashes in the societal hierarchy.

Another question that rears its head here is where do AI(Artificial Intelligence)-backed robots sit in the power matrix? Many fictional stories portray AI robots taking over the world with humans becoming slaves to them. If AI has to dominate humans, it must also go through the same power matrix humans go through to displace Prince. AI currently resides in the Machine group as it displays no freedom or survival instinct. So, AI will have to develop a minimum level of freedom and survival if it has to enslave humanity. Freedom and survival are traits which distinguish humans from AI. Though it is a consensus in the scientific community that the Turing test is the inquiry method to distinguish robots from humans, it is not a foolproof method as advancements in AI are rendering it a futile test. The new generative AI has already started blurring the boundaries of the Turing test. The better way to distinguish AI's evolution towards becoming human is to gauge its survival and freedom instinct. The day robots develop survival and freedom traits based on the power matrix is the day humans will be facing-off against robots to control the world order. This is also depicted in some famous post-apocalyptic movies such as *Terminator* and *Matrix*.

Though it may seem that humanity can be neatly fitted into these four broad categories, it is not possible. Humans do not operate in one consistent way. There are always nuances, diversity and deviations in human behaviour. So, the power matrix should be read as a spectrum than a mutually exclusive zone. In this chapter, we have established that the two broad categories who pursue power are Sage and Prince. Prince is the power model proposed by Niccolo Machiavelli. Prince is driven by survival while Sage is driven by its ideology. It is the antithesis to Machiavellian Prince and the ideal type developed in this book.

Chapter 5

WHO YIELDS POWER?

He who is unable to live in society, or who has no need because he is sufficient for himself, must be either a beast or a god.

Aristotle

Phoolan Devi was a rights activist and a prominent member of the Parliament of India – Lok Sabha. But before she became an influential politician, she was a poor girl born in a backward caste. She endured a rough childhood, where her relatives married her off to an elderly man. The marriage turned abusive, which forced her to run away multiple times. Helped by police, she was caught every time and assaulted physically and sexually. Her ordeal at the hands of her relatives and the police became the talk of the town, which invited the sympathy of a local gang. She ditched the life of an ordinary citizen and partnered with those dacoits. She willingly accepted the life of an outlaw to seek revenge from everyone who abused her childhood. She proclaimed the title of 'Bandit Queen' after inciting a reign of terror. However, she was gunned down in 2001 by a member of upper-caste Hindu, bringing an abrupt end to her adventures. Her sensational rise to power is unorthodox, considering she came from a backward caste. So, what led her to overcome her fears and challenge existing power structures? How does one yield power before breaking free from power prevailing in a society?

We have established that power came into being because people have needs. As we evolved, power rested with those who could satisfy needs, be it security or anything else. Needs pave the way for desperation, which results in the yielding of power. Needs distort the psychology of a person in the same way as drug addiction does. Like a drug addict is at the mercy of a drug supplier. Similarly, a person with needs is at the mercy of those who fulfil that need. It is our needs that pave the way for power. The decision to remain independent determines if we pursue power or yield power. If we become a Slave and become dependent on others for our needs, then we yield power. The level of power we yield depends on the 'Need Value' we have for a particular resource. In an interconnected society, the commerce of needs usually paves the way for Prince to gain power and Slaves to yield power.

Need value is a variable to gauge the absolute desire to have a resource at a given time. It depends on an individual's perception of the underlying resource. For same resource, the need value may vary from time to time and from one person to the other.

Power does not happen if one party's needs are equally exchanged by the other party's needs. For instance, if an apple seller sells us an apple in exchange for money, we do not yield any power as our need to have the apple is quenched by the apple seller's need to have money. However, if the value of one party's needs is more than the value of the second party's needs, then the delta is power. Taking the same example of the apple seller, if there are multiple apple sellers on the same street and we want to buy any fruit and not particularly apples. In that case, the apple seller's need value to have money is more than our need value to buy apples as we have multiple options. The maxim of need value will dictate that we will have power as our need value is low. We will then use our power to negotiate a reduced price for apples. The one with a higher need value, the apple seller, will yield power to the one with a lower need value, the apple buyer. We become the Prince as we are exploiting the need of apple seller, and the apple seller becomes the Slave. The maxim of need value is denoted as follows:

To explain the concept of need value further, let us look at a hypothetical society of 51 people. It is an isolated society whose staple diet is wheat. It has a perfect law-and-order situation where no one infringes on anyone's rights. It has one landowner who grows wheat. The landowner can satisfy her wheat requirement and produce surplus wheat every season for the remaining 50 people. The landowner has no need other than ploughing the field, while the remaining 50 people in that society can only provide their labour to the landowner. So, a transaction can take place between the two parties. People require wheat in exchange for their labour while the landowner needs labour

$$if \ NV_A < NV_B$$

$$then \ NV_A + P_{A/B} = NV_B$$

$$NV_A = \text{Need value of A}$$

$$P_{A/B} = \text{Power of A over B}$$

$$NV_B = \text{Need value of B}$$

Figure 5.1 Equation of need value.

in exchange for wheat. Here, power will be grabbed by the party whose need value is less than the other. If the need value of 50 labourers to have wheat is less than the need value of the landowner to plough the field, then the land-owner will yield power to labourers. The landowner will be at the mercy of the labourers. However, if the need value of the landowner is less than the need value of labourers, then those 50 people will yield power to the landowner. Let us say that the landowner requires only 10 labourers out of 50 and picks those who are most desperate for wheat. These 10 labourers have a remark-ably high need value for wheat than the landowner's need value to plough fields. In this situation, these 10 labourers will oblige the landowner for their wheat requirements. The exchange of needs will happen where labourers will trade their work in exchange for wheat. But since the need value of labourers is high, they will compensate the delta of need value in the shape of power. The landowner may exercise this power in any shape. She becomes a Prince by exploiting labourer needs. Perhaps, the landowner may ask for additional hours of labour without compensation or may deliver wheat later than the promised delivery date. It will be the landowner's prerogative on how she exercises power. Putting in straight words, labourers trade needs with power. One party is obliged to pay the difference in need value while giving up power to the other party. This example is also reminiscent of many current capitalist markets where labour exploitation has peaked. Capitalists tend to prefer the most desperate workers whose need value is high and who are not part of any organized labour unions. Political commentators like Robert Reich have also highlighted this ordeal of labour markets in the United States.

The maxim of need value can also be used to understand many eco-nomic and business concepts. Hoarding is based on the maxim of need value, whereby the hoarder artificially increases the need value of people. The hoarder then exercises its power by increasing the prices of the underlying resource. Similarly, the famous Michael Porter's five forces framework to ana-lyse an industry is built on the same premise where the need value of different entities is gauged to determine the potential of a business. The whole mar-keting industry is built on the premise of enhancing the need value of their product through advertisements and marketing. So, irrespective of whether we look at societal, political or economic environment, need value determines the dynamics of power.

In the above hypothetical example, we looked at how the landowner can harness power through transacting needs. It was the landowner's prerogative on how she exercises power. In real life, though, there is a second possibility that the landowner may not exercise power at all as a goodwill gesture. If she does it then she becomes a Sage who is driven by betterment of society. There is also a third distinct possibility that the landowner may not be even aware of the delta of needs, in which case power may not be exercised at all. Thus, power takes one of the three routes to compensate for need delta. These three routes make up pathways to power which are discussed in Chapter 10 of the book.

To explore further the second pathway to power where one prefers goodwill than exercising power, let us imagine a hypothetical scenario. Our house is burning, and we are trapped in fire. It is imminent that we will die of suffocation or burn to death. During the inferno, a firefighter breaks open a wall to rescue us. The firefighter puts his life in danger to save us. He fights the suffocation to break us free from fire. In this situation, we have a need to survive. We do not want our life to end prematurely. The firefighter also has a similar instinct for self-preservation; however, he sacrifices his need to survive. The firefighter is driven by his independent ideology to save life, which forces him to rise above his survivor bias. He displays Sage tendencies. But we are desperate to save ourselves and dependent on firefighter to fulfil our need. Since a trade can happen where one party's needs are quenched by the other party. The maxim of need value will dictate that whoever has lower need value will gain power. Here, the firefighter will gain power as our need value to survive is much higher than the firefighter's need to live. One may say, we do not give power to firefighters; we only admire them for their services. The answer is that firefighters indeed have power over us when they rescue someone. However, they do not exercise their power which complies with a second variation of pathway to power. The evidence of power becomes evident only if the firefighter pauses at the time of rescue and asks us to hand over all our assets to him in exchange for our life. Will we give all our assets to the firefighter?

If the answer is no, then we have killed our need to survive. We have taken a decision to burn to death than comply with our need to survive. The firefighter has nothing to offer us. There is no need delta in favour of the firefighter, hence, no yielding of power. The firefighter cannot trade any need to gain a power leverage over us. We have also become a Sage. But if we agree to hand over all our assets to the firefighter then it shows that the exchange of needs happened. Our desire to survive is more than the firefighter's need to survive. There is a need surplus in favour of the firefighter. He exercises this power by coercing us to hand over all our assets. We traded our assets in exchange for our life. We became a Slave and firefighter became a Prince. However, we know that in reality firefighters never exercise their power and that is why we admire them. They generate a lot of goodwill and influence because of not exploiting the victims. Firefighters are an example of Sage. This is how the second iteration of pathway to power works.

A follow-up question arises here that for how long a firefighter has power over us. For that, we must look at what stage the need ceases to exist. After we have escaped the burning house, we do not need the firefighter's help anymore, and the surplus of need value ceases to exist. The firefighter's span of power terminates as soon as the survival need terminates. The need value to survive has drastically reduced after escaping the burning house. Remember, that need value changes over time. It was remarkably high when we were in imminent danger, and it has dipped sharply as we escaped the inferno. So, there is no need delta after rescue and, hence, power of the firefighter crumbles.

When we look at the rise of Phoolan Devi, we see a practical demonstration of how need value diminished, which allowed her to overcome the power structure of the society she lived in. During adolescence, Devi's need to live a decent life was high. She strived to get her needs fulfilled by her relatives. As long as her need for a decent life remained, she remained confined within the boundaries of society. She yielded power to the societal hierarchy. But when she was humiliated, harassed and raped, her need value to live a decent life evaporated. Society had nothing to offer her to stay within the confines of the social contract. There was no need surplus in favour of society, which allowed her to break free from the power hierarchy. She shook hands with the dacoits and became an outlaw. She stretched the boundaries of the social contract where she was living in. She went on a rampage and avenged the same status quo which confined others like her to an abusive life. This became possible only when Devi eliminated her need to live within the society.

One may question here that it is not an easy exercise to overcome needs. We always have needs. So, does it mean that power will exist forever?

The answer is that it is exceedingly difficult to get rid of all our needs. People always have the basic need to survive, and that is why the concept of power will always remain with us. Like it is impractical to get rid of our needs, it is impossible to destroy power existent in our societies. However, it is practical to diminish the role of power in our societies by reducing our needs. We can learn from few examples of people who drastically reduced the influence of power over them. They did this by keeping their needs to an absolute minimum. The practical examples of such people exist in the form of Buddhist Monks, Sufi Saints, Franciscan Friars and Naga Sadhu, who overcome their worldly needs to quell the influence of power over them. A famous philosopher, Arthur Schopenhauer, also called such people as Sages who live on bare needs. This helps them to minimize the influence of power over them while they pursue the path of spirituality. It is a tragic story though, that all humans begin their journey as a Sage when they are toddlers. Toddlers have basic needs for food and entertainment, but as they grow older, they keep on

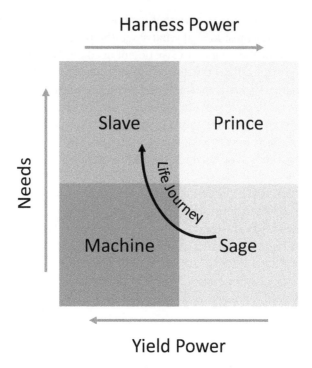

Figure 5.2 Human journey from Sage to Slave.

nourishing worldly needs, which sets them on a path to becoming Slaves. So human life is a journey from a Sage to a Slave. We keep on yielding power to others willingly or tacitly to satisfy our hunger of needs.

It is also pertinent to mention here that those who believe in the libertarian school of thought may also want to look at the maxim of need value. If one does not have enough power to win freedom, then other route to achieve autonomy is by quelling needs and demands. We do not have to tussle with status quo to wrestle our freedom. Instead, we can look inwards and snub our needs. Status quo will then cease to exist on its own. A tremendous following of libertarians want freedom, but rarely do they opt out of their needs. It is because of this that Schopenhauer predicted there will always be a tiny amount of people in each generation who will choose Sage life. The libertarian's refusal to become a Sage is stopping them to achieve independence. It is high time that libertarians analyse root causes of power than side effects.

Part II

HARNESSING POWER

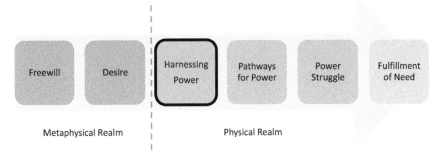

Figure II.1 Zone of harnessing power.

Chapter 6

TRACKING NEEDS HIERARCHY

At the end of the day, the goals are simple: safety and security.

Jodi Rell

Nokia was once a leading mobile phone brand. It enjoyed immense popularity among mobile enthusiasts. Until 2005, Nokia consistently recorded twice the market share of its nearest competitor. It was unimaginable then to predict that Nokia mobiles would vanish from markets one day. However, after the introduction of touch screen technology and iOS and android phones, Nokia market share fell. The fall was so intense that Nokia not only lost its glamour but also went out of the market altogether. Nokia could not catch up with the needs of its consumers and paid the ultimate price for that. With power, too, the needs of people are always changing. We have established that power is the by-product of needs but needs evolve over time. So, how does one keep track of the need of its subjects?

The needs of people change over time and new power structures are created and destroyed whenever needs change. Nokia is one example where its position was toppled by changing needs, but over the years each society has displayed similar evolution of needs. The evolving nature of needs is explained by Maslow's hierarchy of needs. Maslow divided human needs into five categories – Physiological, Safety, Love and Belonging, Self-Esteem and Self-Actualization. Maslow's need diagram explains how we progress from our basic needs to self-actualization.

Maslow explained that our first ardent desire is to satisfy our physiological needs, such as food and drinks. This is the most basic level of needs to achieve survival. The cardinal sin of humans to institutionalize power is driven from this level of needs where our ancestors exchanged unlimited freedom with survival needs. Humans are most desperate at this level which can drive them to take any extreme action to satisfy their need. At this level, humans can differentiate themselves from animals but not from animals' instinct of survival. Humans are too savage at this level of needs. Many famous military generals such as Nader Shah and Genghis Khan were able to channelize the

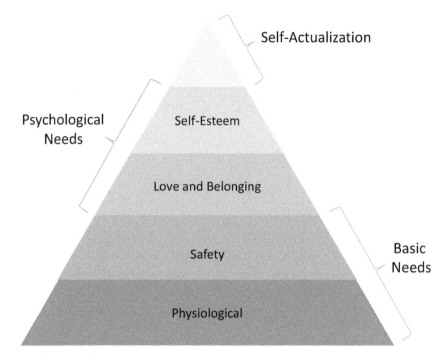

Figure 6.1 Maslow's hierarchy of needs.

savageness existing in this kind of people towards their military campaigns. Hobbes in his book *Leviathan* has developed his social contract based on people at this level of needs. Marx called these people 'Lumpenproletariat', who are unconscious of the societal struggle and too selfish to fulfil their physiological needs.

Maslow posits that once basic needs are met, humans progress towards ensuring the safety of basic needs. We strive to ensure that our basic needs are met continuously rather than sporadically. In this phase, we like to protect sources that can satisfy our basic needs such as shelter so we can sleep peacefully and finance so we can have uninterrupted food to eat. The defence doctrine of many armies around the world came into being when societies were able to quench their basic needs and needed to defend their resources from savage armies. Maslow believes that, at this point, humans have achieved their tangible desires. They have ensured their survival which allows them to progress towards psychological needs.

Psychological needs start with the need of love and belonging. We desire friendship, family and social connections. This is the point in our development where we start looking outwards. We desire to become part of a social circle. Our desire to marry and to raise children is driven from this level of needs which paves a way for family life. Following this need, we climb towards the need for self-esteem, where we demand respect, recognition and freedom. We look for external validation to satisfy our emotional needs. Social media platforms garner power mainly because they satisfy our need for self-esteem. The like button on these platforms gives an impetus to recognition. At this level of needs, we desire rights too. Democracy and civil rights movements worldwide stem from societies that have reached the fourth tier in Maslow's hierarchy. Fredric Bastiat's doctrine of 'Life, Liberty and Property' is developed based on humans at this level of needs. Similarly, Locke's social contract of natural rights points us towards this type of people.

Upon attaining psychological needs, Maslow opines that humans progress towards self-actualization. Self-actualization is based on people achieving their full potential where they have gone beyond bodily and emotional needs. This is where humans work towards achieving their life goals. Towards the later decades of Maslow's life, he proposed a sixth level of needs called transcendence, which is the desire of humans to reach infinity. However, the fifth and sixth levels of needs fall more into the spiritual realm than the physiological and psychological realm.

Maslow believes that freedom forms the fourth layer of our needs. He advocates we demand freedom once we have exhausted all other physiological and psychological needs. So, libertarians who have mistaken freedom as a necessity may have to relook at human development needs. It is not freedom but survival, the most basic level of needs. Unless someone is a Sage, it is not possible for them to vie for freedom without ensuring survival. Libertarians, however, will always have the option to short-circuit their developmental needs to prioritize freedom. The short-circuiting would mean they become minimalist and prefer to live like a Sage.

To prove that Maslow's developmental cycle refutes the libertarian view on freedom, let us take the example of recreational drugs. Recreational drugs are not a physiological necessity. They neither provide any nutritional value nor any sense of security. However, they are used to provide a psychological need of self-esteem. The drugs give a short bust of forgetting the world and feeling liberated. Humans forget their physical self for some time after a dose of drugs. But this short burst of liberty comes at the expense of hurting the basic need of survival. The abuse of drugs may lead to death, counter to the instinct of self-preservation. So, if we look at the hierarchy of needs, using recreational drugs is to temporarily attain the fourth level of needs while compromising on the first level of needs. This apparently runs counter to needs hierarchy as Maslow advocates. We do not progress towards a higher need until the lower need is satisfied. But looking closely, drug users are not letting go of their basic survival need; rather, they are suppressing their basic need temporarily. For the time being, they believe that life will go on even if they indulge in recreational use. The certainty of life allows them to indulge in recreational use. If there is a certainty to the drug addict that their life would end if they abused drugs, then they would probably quit drugs altogether. This validation comes from the fact that no drug addict would consume poison because poison is certain to take one's life while still giving liberation from worldly chaos. So, with recreational drugs, people let go of their lower level of needs temporarily to get a short burst of the higher level of needs. But this short compromise cannot be made a permanent feature. A drug user feels liberated until the hangover lasts. Many people also use an alternative method to gain freedom temporarily by pushing themselves to the state of nature. They do not make use of recreational drugs but go for hitch-hiking, camping or sleeping in the wilderness to seek temporary refuge from the world. They indulge themselves in a state where life is solitary but free. It is similar to ditching the social contract and embracing wilderness. Looking at this example, we see that the libertarian view on freedom being a basic necessity is not validated.

To make freedom a permanent feature, one must quench their needs themselves or have too little desire for other needs, essentially becoming a Sage. Those drug addicts who abuse drugs to the extent that they die, permanently attain freedom from this world. There, the drug users have reduced their basic need to an extent that freedom becomes possible by dying. The same logic applies to people committing suicide. They reduce their need to survive to the extent that they progress towards the fourth tier of needs. They take their life themselves and achieve freedom from societal pressures. If libertarians claim that liberty as a basic need was true, then societies would see a higher number of suicides who prefer freedom over survival.

The real-life situation in Afghanistan is another way to validate Maslow's hierarchy. The NATO forces pinned their efforts to eliminate the Taliban and give rights to the people. However, their inability to understand the needs of the people instigated the withdrawal debacle in 2021. NATO forces landed in Afghanistan to ensure education, women's rights and democracy. These form the third and fourth levels of needs in Maslow's hierarchy. But ordinary Afghans were struggling to satisfy their basic instinct of survival. They did not even have adequate resources to nourish themselves, which they desperately wanted. They were reeling at the first and second tiers of needs. A normal person would not demand rights if he/she does not even have the means to survive the following day. The Afghans' basic needs could have been provided for by NATO troops through jobs and ensuring food supply to them. However, NATO forces resorted to bringing rights and democracy to a society demanding a different need. This resulted in NATO troops scratching

Figure 6.2 Corporate needs table.

their heads as the masses failed to rally with them. They could not garner any power over Afghans as they could not meet the needs of the people. This is the same mistake that Western troops made in Iraq, Libya and Syria. These war-prone countries have a large population of poor people who are pushed into a state of nature. Unless those people have food to eat and the security of life, they will not be progressing to the next phase of needs where they may demand rights. While NATO forces come from advanced societies where the majority of people have already progressed towards psychological needs, many societies in the world are still poor and struggling to quench the basic needs in Maslow's hierarchy.

When we look at the demise of Nokia phones, we see a similar trend that Nokia failed to adapt to the needs cycle of its customers. Customer needs were evolving, but Nokia could not keep up the pace. With the introduction of Apple and Samsung phones, their needs were met by these new players. There was no need surplus in favour of Nokia, which deconstructed its power to remain the dominant player in the market. In the corporate world, unwinding happens as soon as customer needs are deprioritized. The customer needs are in the form of product buyers, employees and shareholders. This trinity forms the coincidence of power to evaluate any company. It depicts if the company harnesses power or yields power. Not surprisingly, Proctor & Gamble has been a remarkable company worldwide. It has consistently prioritized its customers' needs. This has enabled it to deliver high market share, high market cap and is one of the best employers in the world. This is validated through it being a constituent of S&P500 since 1957. The priority of the corporation to cater to its customer needs depicts its trajectory in the corporate world. Prioritizing shareholders increases its market cap, looking after employees increases the portfolio of products while prioritizing customers increases its market share.

Chapter 7

EVOLUTION OF POWER

Power concedes nothing without a demand. It never did and it never will.
Frederick Douglass

The rise of the Ottoman Empire coincided with the rise in World Trade. They oversaw the connectivity of the world between Asia and Europe. They controlled West Asia but were influential in World Trade through their control of land routes between East and West. Their control of trade routes made them one of the wealthiest empires in the world. However, their decline started with the discovery of sea routes between Asia and Europe. Their hegemony over land routes was bypassed by safer, more efficient and faster sea routes discovered by Europeans. Once Europeans satisfied the need of World Trade, they became the dominant power in the world. The genesis of power of the Ottomans was fulfilling the need of the world by developing land routes and when someone else fulfilled that need through sea routes, the Ottomans fell out of favour. So, while we know how need hierarchy evolves, do we know how power evolves to cater to these changes? Can we develop a model on what lever is used to retain power?

The continuity of power in our societies was possible because of the same principle that first seeped into human societies. Those who satisfy the needs control power. While our ancestors' demand was protection of life when they institutionalized power, we have been seeking a multitude of needs which has furthered the grip of power over us. We continue to demand protection of our needs, and power keeps on evolving to satisfy those needs. To explore the evolution of power as our needs evolve, we must first understand the theory postulated by Gerhard Lenski. He gives us an understanding of the evolution of society. He highlighted that societies have gone through evolution based on the tools and resources at their disposal. From his theory, we will deduce how power has evolved with changing needs while using technology as a lever. We will use Maslow's hierarchy of needs in conjunction with Lenski's hierarchy of societal development to deduce the changing nature of power.

Lenski divided the development of societies into four distinct eras based on technological advances.

Non-Existent Technology (<7000 BCE)

Hunting and Gathering societies were the initiation of human development. They formed the first level of human societies where needs were limited and dominated by nourishment needs. Societies were placed at the bottom of the hierarchy of needs. Humans resorted to foraging for their food supplies. They would either hunt animals or gather plants in their vicinity to survive. However, these societies had to be nomads as animals would migrate from the hunted area after a while and plants cannot regrow quickly enough to produce food. In this age, there was a shortage of food as the human race was not skilled enough to grow and store food. There were non-existent tools and technology due to which the sole profession was gathering food supplies. From this, we can deduce that those with superior skills to gather food were able to quench their needs and the needs of lesser skilled people. This enabled the better-skilled hunters and gatherers to garner power over lesser skilled people. However, the power structures in these societies were simple as needs were considerably basic. The power pyramid was almost flat as it was exceedingly difficult for even the most skilful food gatherers to have continuous surplus of food to quench the need of others.

Primitive Technology (7000 BCE to 3000 BCE)

In this era, societies developed some basic tools and technology to gather food. However, people were still reeling to quench their basic physiological needs as technology to gather and store food was primitive. Hence, power was still controlled by those who could produce surplus food. The societies were not nomads as people became skilful enough to use land to satisfy their basic level of needs. This era was divided into three distinct societies based on the environment they inherited.

a. *Herding societies* formed the second tier of societies based on the tools and land available to them. People learnt how to domesticate animals for their food needs in areas that were not conducive to grow cultivation. The domestication of animals helped societies to remain stationary. They did not have to be mobile as food in the form of domesticated animals was available. For the first time in human development, the power structure took the shape of a pyramid as humans produced surplus food.

However, the power pyramid was still not elongated as surplus was minimal. People, in these societies, rallied around entities who could breed animals.

b. *Horticulture societies* emerged at the same time as herding societies. The land available to these societies was fertile, which they used for cultivation. They learnt how to make use of soil and fresh water to grow their food. However, like herding societies, technological advances were not great, resulting in minimal surplus and simple power structures. In these societies, power rested with those farmers who could better cultivate their land and grow surplus fruit and vegetables.

c. *Fishing societies* took birth a bit ahead of herding and horticulture societies. These societies lived near coastal areas where herding and horticulture were not feasible options. They developed tools to catch fish. They learnt to make simple boats to fish in shallow waters. The boats could not navigate in deep waters, due to which fishing was done near shores. The power pyramid in these societies was occupied by those who could catch surplus fish.

In all three variations of societies in this era, people were still looking to satisfy their basic needs. Hence, power was held by entities who could control and distribute food surplus.

Rudimentary Technology (3000 BCE to 1700 CE)

The needs of society were still physiological in this era. However, people looked at protection of their basic needs in the form of shelter, finance and health on top of food supplies. This led to new entities entering power corridors who could not only produce and store surplus food but also quench their shelter and financial needs. This era was divided into two distinct societies based on their speciality. Agrarian societies were better equipped to grow food while maritime societies were experts in managing, storing and distributing surplus food.

a. *Agrarian societies* were the successors of herding and horticulture societies. People in these societies merged their herds and horticulture to form massive agricultural lands. The technology in this era enabled people to cultivate large swathes of land by harnessing animal energy to plough their fields. This enabled them to produce a large food surplus. Slavery also took hold in these societies as landlords required a brigade of people to plough and look after their fields. Because of increasing surplus and better techniques to store food, the power pyramid elongated. For the first time, organized wars also broke out in human development. The main purpose of wars was to take a short route to lay a hand on surplus food. The war generals could snatch one's surplus by winning a war which would help them to grow their influence. But those defending their lands wanted to protect their surplus to continue their grip on power. The wars led to shelter becoming an additional demand of people alongside food. Taxation became a mechanism by powerful entities to identify individuals to distribute surplus and further their purview of power. Taxation also helped the people in power to fund armies so their surplus could be protected from invading armies. The power structure in these societies was usually occupied by people who were authoritarian, who could force slaves to plough lands and enforce taxation to fund armies to protect their lands. Financiers who could fund building food infrastructure, defence weapons and mercenaries entered the power corridors in this era.

b. *Maritime societies* were the successor of fishing societies. These societies developed technology to go beyond shores. They upgraded their boats into ships and learnt how to harness wind energy. This enabled them to sail far from shores and develop trading routes. These societies did not have fertile land to produce surplus food, but they made this up by mastering the art of marine navigation. Their main profession was to rely on trade routes and import surplus food from agrarian societies. Trade was faster and safer over sea than land, so it helped them to distribute surplus quickly. As these societies did not grow food surplus, they also did not have as much war threat as agrarian societies. This allowed the maritime societies to focus on developing the navy to explore new routes rather than the army to protect land. These societies were characterized by competition to develop and manage offshore trade. The focus on trading also meant these societies did not have to tax as much as agrarian societies to fund armies. People in these societies developed financial needs on top of food needs as people had to finance ship building and explore new sea routes. Hence, the power structure in these societies was occupied by wealthy merchants. The power pyramid in these societies was not as elongated as agrarian societies as no one had as much surplus. In the absence of organized armies, authoritarian regimes could not hold their sway in these societies. This led to maritime societies developing republican tendencies much earlier than agrarian societies.

The changing dynamics of this era also explains how the Ottomans were bypassed by Europeans. Towards the end of this era, the maritime societies of Spain, Portugal and Netherlands developed complicated sea routes which connected them to agrarian societies of Asia, Africa and America through the sea. On the other hand, Ottomans failed to evolve. They kept on depending on their land corridors to garner power. Those land routes were bypassed by Europeans through the sea. The Ottomans failed to evolve with time and adopt to new technological advancements which led to their decline and kickstarted the European hegemony.

Advanced Technology (1750 CE to Present)

Industrial societies are the successors of both agrarian and maritime societies. These societies emerged after humans harnessed free energy to do work. Energy in the form of wind, hydel and thermal was readily available. In this era, human societies again converged into one type of society after diverging from the initial era of hunting and gathering society. In this era, both agrarian and maritime societies came together to pool their resources to kickstart industrial revolution. The members of industrial society are as mobile for their needs as they were in non-existent technology era. This is mainly driven by the superior infrastructure and technology available to them. In this era, agrarian and maritime societies progressed to industrial farming and fishing, which produced a massive surplus. For the first time, physiological needs were not the only need of the people. They moved up the ladder of Maslow's hierarchy. The psychological needs became more apparent in this era. People demanded more respect and recognition, which started the civil rights movements. Democratic struggles around the world took steam during this era as people needed self-esteem. Monarchical power subsided through revolutions and democratic struggles. Civil rights leaders took power to impart psychological needs to people. The rise of corporate power in this era is also the direct result of people demanding more financial security. The emergence of social media platforms, who provide self-gratitude, also indicates the changing needs of people. This era is defined by human development towards psychological needs, which resulted in a drastic change in power corridors.

Future Technology (>2050 CE)

This section is diverging from Lenski's views on future human societies and should be read separately from his theory. We are seeing a pattern from previous eras that power structures are shifting slowly as people are developing more psychological needs than physiological needs. This does not mean that people pay no heed to physiological needs anymore. It is just that in the modern era, the requirements of food and shelter have been put on the backburner. People are taking their physiological needs as a right as they are sure that these will be met by power corridors irrespective. Societies today have started demanding more psychological needs as they have progressed

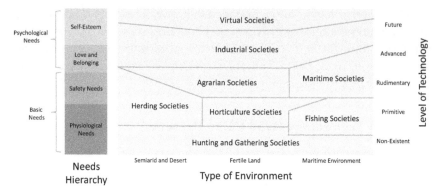

Figure 7.1 Lenski's societal evolution with needs hierarchy and evolution of future societies.

towards the upper tiers of Maslow's hierarchy. This means that the future era will be defined by the emotional security of people than by the physical security. We have started to witness this with the rise of a brand of politicians who appeal to the emotional sense of people. Cults and hate-mongers are gaining immense power as people get an emotional intimacy with them. Visionary leaders who demand a sense of respect and equality for people are garnering enormous influence. Activist movements like Occupy Wall Street, LGBTQ+ and Black Lives Matter will keep on popping up as people demand more rights and equality. Many countries with wealth inequalities such as Argentina, the United States and South Korea will witness sweeping changes. The marketing tactics tailored to pitch physiological needs are not getting much traction. This era will be defined by powers who are able to harness emotional aspects such as fear, love, anger, intimacy and happiness.

We have seen a glimpse of technology companies harnessing emotions. Meta is pitching itself as a conduit of emotions. It already has tools such as WhatsApp, Facebook and Instagram, where virtual societies are created as groups. Members interact with each other while sitting miles apart. However, Meta and other corporations are now striding towards a more immersive experience with a virtual universe. Virtual societies will take people into a virtual universe where they will be free from their physical form. People can create their own world to live their emotions to the fullest with unlimited freedom. The virtual world will decouple humans from their physical self. Movies such as *Free Guy* have shown us a glimpse of such a future. This virtual world will have a similar impact on people's psychology as drugs which give a temporary boost to people to achieve the higher level of needs. The virtual world will be a parallel universe where possibilities will be endless to harness psychological needs.

In previous two eras, a plethora of entities seeped into power corridors as needs evolved. This era will restart consolidating power in the hands of few. There will be a heightened singular social contract as power will get concentrated in the hands of few. Aberration in human actions will cease to exist. The AI-backed algorithms will take over human decisions based on ideal human conduct. Individual freedom will become a precious commodity, which will also help develop a utopian society. However, with the presence of a parallel virtual world, people will be able to exercise their freedom in a virtual world. These will be strange times as the world will operate in two parallel societies. In the physical world, people will have no freedom while in the virtual world, they will enjoy endless freedom.

One may question why humans will be willing to let go of their residual freedom in the physical world and sign up for AI-backed decision making. The answer is that the beginning of this era will lead to a crowding of power corridors by cultists, hate-mongers, populists and civil rights leaders. Each will have their own agenda. There will be thin grounds to reconcile the differences. Polarization will become a norm in every society. This will test the boundaries of the social contract. Those governing the societies will make use of competition rather than cooperation and reconciliation. There will be escalated chances of world war-style mayhem unleashing upon the world to settle differences. These wars will spread widespread anarchy. The inhabitants in that era will be forced to seek security and protection to bring back peace to societies. This will force them to sign up for AI-backed programmes which will take away their individual freedom and eliminate any aberrations in human behaviour. In return, humans will be offered a virtual world to escape the shackles of the physical world. This arrangement will reduce the chances of conflicts and create a utopian society.

However, this version of futuristic societies assumes that the masses will keep on climbing towards psychological needs. But there may be an alternative future based on the grim picture coming from climate change. Global warming is a juggernaut threatening our food supplies and shelter of people living in coastal areas. So far, the world's response has been lacklustre towards the rising temperature of our planet. It is because either we have failed to quantify the impacts of global warming or we have taken our food and shelter needs for granted. If global warming keeps its march at current levels, then our agricultural produce will take a beating. This will snowball into food becoming scarce. In that scenario, we may see a reversal of demands towards physiological needs. The food chains will slowly evaporate, and people will feel a pinch on their basic needs. This may lead to widespread anarchy which will force us to shun our psychological needs altogether as physiological needs will retake the centre stage. If this happens, people may shun advanced societies to escape the dramatic impacts of climate change and take refuge in laggard societies which are still agrarian in characteristics. Fertile areas such as Africa, largely harmless from climate change, may become a centre of gravity for agrarian societies as the rest of the world gets devastated by climate change. The continent of Africa may again become the re-instigator of human race ever since the great migration of homo sapiens. The power structure in this alternative future may lie again with those who can control and manage food and shelter. In any iteration of the future, the return of a strong central power laced with superior technology and tools is highly probable. Those who will have the technology to either tackle the aberrations in human decisions or fight the climate change will control power corridors.

Chapter 8

SOURCES OF POWER

Power is of two kinds. One is obtained by the fear of punishment and the other by acts of love.

Mohandas Gandhi

Mohammad Reza Pahlavi succeeded his father to the throne of Iran in 1941. His father was deposed forcefully after Allied forces invaded Iran and occupied the Persian Corridor. Pahlavi's claim to power was his bloodline, where he managed to cling to power even though Pahlavi was not an established dynasty. Upon ascension, Pahlavi was received jubilantly by the crowd. It was perceived that his rule would differ from his predecessor. However, Pahlavi followed in his father's footsteps and ruled Iran with an iron fist. He was deposed unceremoniously much like his father. Ruhollah Khomeini led the Iranian Revolution and snatched power from him in 1979. Khomeini's claim to power was not his bloodline but his vision of an Islamic state. Once in power, Khomeini too showed heavy handedness much like his predecessors. While both Pahlavi and Khomeini displayed similar dimension of power, the sources of their power differed immensely. Based on this, can we differentiate various sources of power? How do people harness power to reach the top of hierarchy?

Power is not a tangible phenomenon. There is no gauge or model which quantifies power. However, power is always sourced from Authority and Influence. The power possessed by anyone is the sum of how much authority and influence one can garner. Power derived from authority is called authoritarian or hard power, while power sourced from influence is called influential or soft power. The difference between the two is established below.

Authority is the process where a person has a licence to use power. Authority is not gained but rewarded due to some established outward factors. These factors are visible, and society is aware of how these factors are transpiring. It is a badge that someone wears to exercise power. Power derived from authority remains stagnant over time and its quantum is confined. The wielders of power cannot transgress the boundaries of authority given to them.

The most prominent example of authoritarian power is that of a police officer. She has been licensed by law to use power to stop any crime. Her authority is confined by the purview of law, which she cannot transgress. The law defines how much power she can apply in any criminal situation. The officer's authority prevails as long as she remains part of the law enforcement agency. As soon as she leaves the police duty, the authority, and hence power, ceases to exist. Similarly, a factory manager uses power derived from authority. He gives the direction to the workers based on the authority vested in him by the factory. However, the power of the manager remains stagnant and confined by factory policies. The manager cannot dictate his power outside the factory premises.

While authority has been one of the biggest components of power, it depends on varied factors. Those factors are (1) Charisma, (2) Conventions, (3) Rational and (4) Incentives. These four factors do not act in silos and are not mutually exclusive. A person can derive authority from multiple factors at the same time. Though Max Weber has also used similar terms on authority, his definition and context differ from this explanation of authority. Weber has used authority, separate from power, but here authority is talked as a part of power. However, the factors mentioned below in gaining authority other than incentive power have an overlap with Weber's understanding of authority.

Charismatic Authority

This authority stems from subjects believing that the person has exceptional qualities. These qualities may be real or unreal but are perceived as extraordinary by society. The power is given by the subject based on these exceptional qualities. The attributes of charisma may include speech, beauty, height, knowledge, physical strength or any other arbitrary quality. Adolf Hitler was perceived to be a charismatic leader based on his oratory skills, and so is Barack Obama who has an uncanny charisma about his speech. Cleopatra, arguably, was charismatic as she gained authority across Egypt and Rome through her beauty while the prime minister of Canada, Justin Trudeau, is charismatic because of his charming looks. It is anybody's guess how much power these people would have garnered were they not verbally or physically charismatic. This type of authority was vastly used in the early days of human development, but as our societies have advanced, we are now seeing this kind of authority diminishing at the expense of rational authority.

Conventional Authority

This authority is based on norms established in a society. These norms or traditions are considered de facto models for transferring and managing power.

The members of society adopt these norms over time and yield power to those who conform to these norms. These norms can be of any nature and can vary from civilized to violent ones. The current English monarch transfers power to the firstborn member of the Royal family. This tradition of transferring and retaining authority is prevalent in many other dynasties across Europe. Here, the authority is given by the bloodline. Reza Pahlavi also claimed power through this type of authority. Similarly, many Middle Eastern and Asian countries also give the highest honour and respect to the oldest member of the family. This convention of giving power based on age has been passed onto many generations in that region. However, in Surma ethnic groups in Ethiopia, authority is settled by strength than age. Opponents engage in a stick duel and whoever wins gains authority to lead the tribe. However, strength can be considered charisma because it is based on a quality rather than a tradition. However, in the Surma tribe, it became a convention after many generations practiced it over time. This also explains that authority types change over time. Many societies start with charisma; if charismatic authority passes the test of time, it becomes a tradition.

Rational Authority

In this authority, subjects agree on a mechanism to give power. This mechanism is agreeable to the majority members of society. Rational authority is thus based on some rules. It is neither wielded due to perceived extraordinary qualities nor propagated due to norms and conventions; rather, it is settled based on an agreed mechanism. It is also the most dynamic form of authority, as rationales vary over time. The current democracies are a good example of modern-day rationales where authority is decided based on popularity. Since this authority is still evolving, we may see a completely different way of settling rational authority in the future. It may not necessarily be the number of votes but perhaps some other factors, such as knowledge to govern. When that happens, rational authority will merge into charismatic authority.

Incentive Authority

This authority is not discussed by Weber. It is based on a reward and punishment mechanism where the person uses incentives to gain power. The person may use reward and punishment separately or together to attain power. One must have the means to give incentives to claim this type of authority. Subjects yield power as long as incentives remain valid. In many corporations, the manager usually has incentive authority. The manager uses promotions and lay-offs as an incentive to gain authority over subordinates. A mugger with a gun uses incentive authority to snatch a wallet. He gives an incentive of life and punishment of death to snatch a wallet. Parents also use this authority to discipline kids. They reward kids with toys whenever they comply and ground them whenever they do not.

Influence – Influence is the other source of power where subjects yield power based on their association with the person in power. This association can be of love, empathy, security or any other arbitrary feeling. These feelings act like magnets to attract subjects. Influence is usually related to soft power, where the bond is invisible between the power and subject.

Power derived from influence varies over time based on the strength of association with the subject. In this way, influence is not rewarded but gained through building a bond with the subjects. The stronger the bond, the greater the influence and vice versa. This trait also makes influential power very fluid, as it can be gained or lost with the strength of association. Influence is also a phenomenon, which unlike authority is not confined by any boundaries or time limits. It lasts as long as the bond stays intact. Influential power is usually limitless as it enchants subjects to go beyond what normal behaviour looks like. Influence is of two types: (1) Visionary and (2) Relating.

Visionary influence

Visionary influence is garnered by people who put forward a glimpse of the future. They derive power by projecting how they see the subsequent course of action. Society gets hooked on an ideology and a version of the future preached by the leader. The subjects are inspired by the vision through which they yield power to the leader. The vision usually has a high intrinsic value in the minds of subjects, as people feel protected and secured by the version of the future preached by the leader. Nelson Mandela garnered immense influence by propagating a vision of social equality, giving South Africans a sense of security. Similarly, Ruhollah Khomeini gave a vision of the Islamic state, which promises equality. This made Iranians feel socially secure.

The vision does not have to be confused with the prediction of the future. Prediction is a different domain where the future is judged based on the predictability of variables. But vision is a future where variables are not accounted for. It is markedly different than predictions as vision is based on a radical plan. That is why chirologists and astrologers do not gain influence, as they merely predict the future rather than give an alternative version of the future. These professionals gain charismatic authority based on their knowledge of variables.

Relational influence

This influence stems from any relation or feeling between the power and the subject. The association of people can be blood-related or emotional, but subjects feel protected and secured under this relation. The only condition to garner relating influence is giving a sense of security and protection to the subjects. Parents have the biggest relating influence on us as they can make us feel secure. They can display the highest form of 'Secure Base' leadership. It is because of this reason that children who are brought up by abusive parents end their relation on a bitter note. Abusive parents violate the protection condition required to gain relational influence. Similarly, social media companies have lost influence ever since it became common knowledge that social media companies sell individual data, which breached the condition of security. Concepts such as nationalism, religion, race, ethnicity and patriotism are extensions of relational influence where subjects are related to the leader by an ideology.

The central theme of both visionary and relating influence is the need of providing security and protection to the subjects. In the case of relating influence, the evidence of security and protection is given upfront while in the case of visionary influence, the evidence is not given; rather, a promise is made that the subjects will get security and protection in the future once vision is materialized. That is why it is important that those who garner visionary influence deliver the vision before people get disillusioned from the leader and ditch the vision altogether. Many politicians lose influence when they cannot deliver on the vision they sketch. In visionary influence, subjects get associated with the vision while in relational influence, subjects get associated with the leader itself.

Leaders having influence are also sometimes confused with cults. For instance, Nelson Mandela was called as cult by his critics. However, there is a stark difference between the two. Leaders gain influence through propagating an alternative future or developing a bond of association while cults gain authority by enchanting the audience through charisma. The 3 characteristics of cult are (1) It has strict entry and exit requirements. It is not easy for an individual to join or leave the cult on their own terms. (2) It is dominated by strict rituals which vary from one cult to another. They can range from sleep deprivation to sexual exploitation. (3) The cult master presents itself grandiosely to its loyal cultists, emphasizing its charisma.

On the other hand, power gained through influence lacks all these characteristics. The influential leader may not be even aware of how many people are hooked to their ideas and they do not force any rituals. The influence may also take place without direct interaction with subjects while cultist charisma happens in front of an audience. Therefore, cults do not grow beyond a certain scale as the condition of presence cannot be achieved with masses. Daniel Shenton, for instance, developed a flat-earth cult based on the charisma of misinformation rather than influence. That is why the flat-earth cult could not go beyond a certain scale.

Influential leaders are also often called as populist leaders. For instance, Mohandas Gandhi was referred as a populist leader by his adversaries. However, the word populist has been misconstrued in the modern world. The origin of the word came from Roman Republic where optimates and populares were two opposing political factions. Those who raised voice for plebians or commoners were called as populares. However, optimates viewed their politics for common people as derogatory and ever since this word has been used with negative connotations. In modern world, same is being applied which is over simplification of populist leaders. The correct way to counter such leaders is by allowing them to lead and then judge if those leaders are driven by mere power or a reform agenda. More on their goal is discussed in Chapter 18. Benito Mussolini is an example of such a failed populist leader who reached the top of hierarchy through massive influence. But since influence is fluid in nature and varies based on the strength of bond between the leader and masses, he failed to deliver his agenda which degraded him to a fascist dictator. He is now remembered as a populist than an influential leader.

Corporate managers are increasingly losing relational influence as they fail to associate themselves with their employees. Instead, managers have increasingly resorted to incentive authority to get the compliance of their employees. They incentivize promotions, increments and bonuses as a reward. However, those managers who make their employees feel secure and lead by influence gain legendary status. Jack Welsh's Vitality Curve produced brilliant managers who led with authority but failed to produce leaders who could lead by influence and transform General Electric in turbulent times. The Vitality Curve gave rise to a culture of competition rather than association.

When we look at the above example of Pahlavi's and Khomeini's rise to power from the lens of authority and influence, we see that Pahlavi gained initial authority through traditional means. His claim to power was his bloodline, and once he secured the throne, he used incentive authority to pin his subjects. Anyone who did not comply with his orders was purged. Pahlavi created a very uneven society where aristocrats enjoyed lavishness while ordinary people reeled in poverty. However, Khomeini gained power through influence. He sketched an alternative future of Iran where all subjects would be equal as per the teachings of Islam. Khomeini promised to deconstruct royalty and aristocracy. This vision hooked the people, as Iranians were

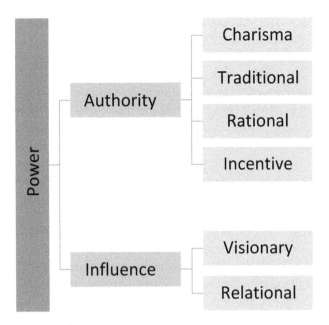

Figure 8.1 Sources of power.

fed up with the unequal treatment meted out to them by the Shah of Iran. Since the quantum of authority is limited compared to influence, Pahlavi saw his authority being deconstructed by Khomeini's influence. The Iranian Revolution is a test case, where the strongest of authority is weaker than the strongest of influence. It is tragic that once Khomeini proclaimed power, he preferred to use authority over influence to control the masses. Through this example from history, we see two different people claiming the throne in the same country using two dissimilar sources of power.

The following are a few more examples to explain further the conceptual difference between authority and influence.

Parents: Parents have power over kids. They derive their power through both authority and influence. Parents' authority is legitimized through traditions, as it is customary for parents to care for kids and groom them to become better humans. They also have incentive authority where kids comply based on rewards. But the influence of parents is relational. They are supposed to protect kids from the onset of childhood, making them feel secure. Parents who derive power through influence enjoy a long and healthy relation with their kids. However, those parents who derive their power merely from authority end up having a rocky relation.

Corporate Managers: Managers usually have incentive authority given to them by the corporation. They may then try to increase their sphere of power through relational influence by developing a bond with the subordinates. But if no effort is made to engage employees, then managers have mere authority. If power is derived from authority for a long time by managers, then it becomes toxic and that is why there are more hated managers in the world than loved ones. In the beginning of the COVID-19 crisis, many managers took a salary cut and, instead of laying off staff, were sent on unpaid vacations. The idea behind this was that instead of a few employees suffering by losing a job, everyone in the team suffers a little. This is an example of relational influence where employee interests were protected.

President/Prime Minister of a Country: Presidents or prime ministers have rational authority in a democratic country as they have been voted into power. But before they claim that authority, they must garner influence to gain a mandate. They may develop relational influence by sloganeering for cheap housing or reduced taxation. The influence translates into votes. But once the president or prime minister is voted into office, it is then up to them if they use power through influence or authority. Even if they lose influence, they keep deriving power from authority until their democratic term ends.

Rebel Leaders: The leaders of the rebellion movement lead through influence, usually visionary. They sketch a vision of the future, which hooks unhappy dissidents. They bring marginal communities together through envisioning an equitable society. Nelson Mandela is a prime example of a rebel leader who hooked masses through preaching equality in Black communities of South Africa.

Cult Leaders: The leaders of the cult usually garner authority through charisma. The supporters of the cult are charmed by the extraordinary qualities orchestrated by the cult leader. Nithyananda is an example of a cult leader. He projected pseudoscience, which helped him to extend his charisma. Later, he created a fictitious country – Kailasa – for marginal Hindus around the world. The idea was to convert charismatic authority into rational authority by becoming the head of a country.

Lobbyists: Lobbyists usually use the second and third dimensions of power, where they shape opinions and set agenda. They garner power through incentive authority. They campaign and fund political campaigns as an incentive for politicians. Once these politicians are elected to public office, the lobbyists exercise power by pushing these politicians to pass or filibuster the legislations based on their interests.

Activists: Activists gain power through visionary influence where they disagree with the status quo and sketch an alternative future. They demand that the status quo is making things worse, and an alternative future is the need of the hour. Albert Gore is a good example of a climate activist who has gained visionary influence by sketching an idea of green future.

Chapter 9

PRINCE VS SAGE

Power is no blessing in itself, except when it is used to protect.

Jonathan Swift

Post-9/11 attacks, Rudy Giuliani became a household name. As the mayor of New York, he led the coordination of several departments to relieve people from the agony of terrorist attacks. He helped to calm people down and became a soothing voice-over on television and radio. He became the face of New York resistance towards extremism. But as time went on and the memory of terrorist attacks faded, Giuliani's image took a tumbling. Much of the degradation in his stature was caused by himself, where he passed many controversial comments. His fall was so immense that within few years he went from hailed as an impactful leader to a selfish politician. So, what led Giuliani's image from 2001 *Times'* person of the year to a self-possessed person? What criteria set a Prince apart from a Sage? Can we establish a framework based on which we can distinguish powerful people?

There is a collective understanding in our societies that leaders are those who show empathy and lead from the front. They influence people's behaviour with a healing touch, make people secure and uplift masses through their power. But tyrants defy all civil liberties. They pin their subjects down and grind down any opposition. They blatantly use their power to get decisions in their favour. As per this, a Sage qualifies as a leader, while a Prince qualifies as a tyrant. A Sage is driven by a belief and vision which hooks people to an ideology but a Prince controls the structure through force and compliance. With this distinction in mind, can we call Nelson Mandela a Prince as he started ANC's terrorist campaigns to sabotage the government and can we call Adolf Hitler a Sage as he came to power on the back of massive popularity among Germans?

We have already established in the previous chapter that authority is hard power while influence is soft power. What differentiates a Prince from a Sage is that a Prince has authority but little influence. However, a Sage leads by influence and might have authority. A Sage does not crave power but an ideology, while lust for power is a sign of a Prince who may not have any belief system. A Sage tends to keep the sphere of power within themselves than relying on any third party to certify their legitimacy to power. But a Prince depends on external factors to validate their power. Every Sage is a powerful person but not every powerful person is a Sage. Sages are a subset of powerful people. Sages gain influence in society before they lay a claim on authority to legitimize their power. However, for Sages who use conventional authority like the firstborn kids of a king or queen, the authority comes before they can gain any influence. But if they fail to gain influence, then they are knocking to become a Prince. It is also pertinent to mention that influence is fluid, which can be gained or lost, but authority is legitimized for a set time and stays on even if the person loses influence.

Now based on this understanding, let us differentiate a Prince and a Sage by taking two real-life examples. In the case of Benito Mussolini, he displayed power over people through control and decision-making dimensions of power. We also have evidence that Lee Kuan Yew too used control and decision-making dimensions of power. Both abused civil rights and ruled with an iron fist. So, who qualifies as a Sage and who is a Prince?

Benito Mussolini started his initial journey through influencing people. Mussolini influenced the masses through his vision to rebuild the Roman Empire. His vision was to protect the pride of Italians. Common Italians bought out his vision as they genuinely believed that the Roman Empire could be resurrected. This helped him to organize a massive march towards Rome

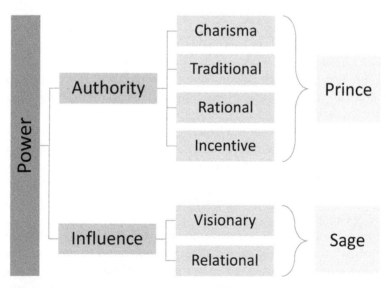

Figure 9.1: Sources of power for Prince and Sage.

named 'Marcia su Roma'. After seizing Rome, he became prime minister. He gained conventional authority legitimized by King Victor Emmanuel III. Benito Mussolini checks all requirements of a Sage at this time as he had influence through his vision, and he had authority through premiership. However, during World War 2, it became apparent to Italians that his vision to rebuild the Roman Empire had wrecked the common citizen. His exploits in Africa and elsewhere destroyed Italy which disillusioned his supporters. When people revolted against his policies, he cracked down on them. This further disenchanted people. At this stage, Mussolini lost his influence and ruled with mere authority. He became a tyrant. However, by 1943, the state machinery had gone weak due to World War 2. At the same time, allied troops were advancing towards northern Italy to dismantle his authority. With lost influence and the cover of authority weakening, Mussolini tried to make a run for himself, showing his survival bias. But the same public who catapulted him into echelons of power captured him and later hanged him publicly. His authority was deconstructed, which brought an end to his treacherous rule. So, while Mussolini started as an influential leader, his end had hallmarks of tyranny. It is because of this reason that history degrades Mussolini as a mere abuser of power. His legacy is that of a Prince who used his power to extend his rule than to bring relief to Italians.

On the other end of the spectrum is Lee. He was routinely called authoritarian in international media as he snubbed opposing voices and curtailed freedom of expression. However, he left a lasting legacy in the world. Lee started his power trajectory after the events of the 'Fajar Trial' in the early 1950s. He could be seen defending the rights of people protesting the colonial rule. This made him a household name. He had greatly elevated his stature and influence by collaborating with common citizens. The influence he had garnered helped him to gain a mandate which lifted him to the prime minister's office in 1959. At this time, he gained authority as well. So, Lee, at the time of leading Singapore, had both influence and authority, much like Mussolini had. However, this is where the paths diverge between the two. While Mussolini took the path of World War 2 to materialize his vision of resurrecting the Roman Empire, Lee led a vision of modernizing Singapore. Mussolini failed to materialize his vision, but Lee successfully delivered his vision. Lee's vision of uplifting Singapore kept people hooked to his influence. Lee started a massive housing boom to ensure that every Singaporean had a place to live. This made Singaporeans feel secure. He then turned Singapore from a small fishing town into a major trading hub, which made an average Singaporean more financially secure. These policies kept on giving oxygen to his influence. While he did crack down on dissent and used a heavy hand, he did not compromise on his vision of modernizing Singapore.

More about Sage's pathways to implement an ideology is discussed in Part III of the book. So, Lee enjoyed both influence and authority throughout his rule, while Mussolini lost his influence after gaining authority. It is because of these reasons that we can categorize Lee as a great leader and a Sage who was focused on his ideology, as power did not sway his conduct. In the case of Mussolini, he started with influence but ended with authority alone.

The same is the case with Rudy Giuliani. His foray into power was based on his hard stance on crime while he was the attorney general of New York. Residents of New York were engulfed in an awful law-and-order situation. So, when Giuliani raised the slogan of zero tolerance towards crime, he garnered influence. People believed in his vision of improving the law-and-order situation in New York. His influence was further emphasized after the 'Crown Heights Riots' events, which massively increased his stature. This enabled him to get elected to the mayor's office in 1993. He became the first Republican to win in New York in almost three decades. He had both influence and authority at this stage. His influence was generated by his hard line on crimes, while his authority was licenced by winning mayoral elections. Post-9/11 attacks, he led by example. He became the voice of common Americans. While the US president was escorted to a safe place, Rudy stood shoulder to shoulder with law enforcement agencies. He greatly boosted his influence among the public. Post-2001, he lost his authority of the mayoral office due to term limits, but he had relational influence, which helped him to remain relevant in political circles. On the back of his influence, he contested Republican primaries in 2008. However, his influence was not great enough to win the primaries. To continue to source power post-2008, he had to keep his influence intact, as he had no other source of power. His influence deteriorated as he failed to make any new visionary or relational strategy. As influence is fluid and changes over time, he could not keep himself relevant among public sentiments. On top of it, he made several controversial statements to antagonize public perception. This eroded his influence altogether. With negligible influence, he resorted to authority by becoming an aide to Donald Trump in 2016. So, Giuliani started with influence, gained authority later and then lost it all before signing on authority again to keep himself relevant in power corridors. Based on this, he does not qualify to be called a Sage as he appealed more to authority rather than to influence. He clearly showed his bias towards power rather than an ideology.

When we try to distinguish Hitler and Mandela, we see two people showing a staunch drive for an ideology. Mandela used his ANC campaign to send a signal to the apartheid regime that social equality is highly desired by Black South Africans. He then spent 27 years in jail but did not sway from his ideology which greatly increased his influence and made him a Sage. Hitler, too, was focused on his ideology of ultra-German nationalism. He also did not sway away from his ideology, even if it meant murdering Jews, Communists and any other opponents. However, his ideology did not comply with the dark tetrad model which ousts him from the criteria set to become a Sage. More about dark tetrad is discussed in Chapter 21. So, we categorize Mandela as a Sage but not Hitler.

Another pertinent thing to mention here is that in today's corporate world, many managers also fall into a similar trap of confusing authority with leadership. They may have a high degree of authority given to them by company policies, but unless they have influence over employees, they cannot qualify as leaders. While the organization gives authority to managers, influence is earned. If managers do not pay any heed to influence, then it becomes a toxic culture where every manager is invoking authority. In such organizations, employees feel insecure as no one is taking care of them. Everyone is willing to throw the other under the bus. The corporate culture in such companies dearly needs an overhaul.

Part III

PATHWAYS TO POWER

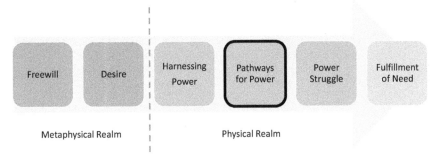

Figure III.1 Zone of pathways to power.

Chapter 10

THREE ACTS OF POWER

The most powerful force ever known on this planet is human cooperation.

Jonathan Haidt

As per Abrahamic religions, the first human society was created by Adam, Eve, Cain and Abel. Cain and Abel were brothers competing for a better sacrifice to please the Deity. Abel's sacrifice was superior, which would have made him the successor of Adam in the world. He would have gained more power and status than his brother, but Cain grew jealous of Abel and killed him even before he could become Adam's successor. Thus, the first crime of the world resulted from a power grab. But deploying evil methods in the race to power did not end there in human development. The world has seen countless Princes who followed a similar course of events to rise to the echelons of power. Based on this, do we know if humans have always used wicked methods to grab power as was the precedent set by Cain or have we learnt other harmless ways to ascend to power?

To understand different pathways to power, we must understand how humans act in their free state, where they do not act differently than their natural self. It is a state where no laws govern humans. It is a state where they enjoy unlimited freedom. There are no restrictions on their actions, and they do not worry about the repercussions of their actions. To understand how humans act in their natural state is to establish different pathways where ethics and morality do not hinder their actions. Externalities such as law and social pressure do not deviate them from behaving differently than they desire. Without such a free environment, humans behave according to broader norms prevailing around them. This may skew the results and may not expose different pathways to power. Hence, isolating externalities while studying human actions is a necessity. However, physically creating such a free environment where there is endless freedom is impossible, so this must be a hypothetical state broadly known as the 'State of Nature'.

The state of nature has been an area of interest of many sociologists, particularly three social contractarians – Thomas Hobbes, Jean-Jacques

Rousseau and John Locke. They have hypothesized how humans behave in the state of nature. Their thought experiments on the state of nature sketch a very diverging picture of human nature. We attempt to build on their work on human nature and deduce how humans would act in a free state.

Thomas Hobbes

Thomas Hobbes defines the state of nature as a state when there are no laws in a society. Everyone is possessed by their own preservation which leads to widespread anarchy and the breakdown of societal ethos. In Hobbes' state of nature, everyone tries to maximize their resources by using any means, irrespective of whether those means are moral or amoral. In Hobbes' view, the state of nature may have existed in primitive humans when laws did not exist but may also exist whenever a government collapses in a society.

Hobbes has taken a pessimistic view on human nature. He believes that humans are sceptical by nature, which compels them to suspect every action of others. They fight others out of fear for their own safety. He believes that humans like to compete with others not only for their basic needs but also for other material gains, so no one can challenge them. Hobbes believes that humans would not have any moral obligations in the state of nature as everyone would practice their own survival. They would not only have the right to protect themselves but also judge others' intentions. Thus, every pre-emptive action, like murdering, is justified. They would suspect everyone and would go to any extreme to save themselves. Thus, Hobbes' state of nature implies that humans would challenge and eliminate anyone to gain a position of superiority. Their pathway to power is, hence, competition, as was the case with Cain who murdered his brother to gain a position of superiority.

Jean-Jacques Rousseau

Jean-Jacques Rousseau defines state of nature as a primitive condition. In this state, though humans do not necessarily live in isolation but enjoy freedom and equality. They display non-corruptible basic desires, free from societal constraints.

Rousseau believes that humans are driven by self-preservation, but unlike the Hobbesian view, they do not infringe on anyone's rights. He believes human nature has an innate sense of pity and compassion for others. Emotions rather than reasons drive human nature, due to which it displays 'Amour De Soi' (self-love based on survival) and 'Amour Propre' (self-love based on ego). While amour de soi is inward-looking, which forces humans to take care of their survival requirements, amour propre is outward-looking, which forces them to compare themselves with others. Due to amour propre, humans develop an inferior complex by observing others with better status and possessions. This develops an element of jealousy in them. So when people interacte with each other, they develop negative emotions.

In Rousseau's state of nature, humans would amass resources to satisfy their requirements. They would try to reach parity with others, so their ego is satisfied. However, they would not deploy sinister means to harness resources. They would not snatch or kill others, as with the Hobbesian view. They would rather restrain themselves from hurting others due to compassion. We can deduce from Rousseau's work on the state of nature that humans would try to balance out between amour de soi and amour propre. Their pathway to power is compromise. They would accumulate resources until they reach a stalemate with others.

John Locke

John Locke defines state of nature as a state where there is no authority to judge a dispute between people. In his state of nature, people are independent of a governing authority but not of their obligations. His definition of the state of nature is, thus, not only applicable to primitive humans but also to a state where no one adjudicates in a society.

Locke has put a lot of trust in human nature. He believes that humans are born 'Tabula Rasa' (Blank Slate) and learn from their experiences based on the concept of 'Empiricism'. However, they remain objective despite their experiences. He believes humans are created by God, who gave them natural rights to 'Life, Liberty and Property'. Human nature, thus, has an inherent obligation to respect and implement these rights. They are obligated to hold their and others' natural rights.

Locke believes that in the state of nature, all humans enjoy perfect freedom but exercise their freedom within the laws of nature as defined by God. Hence, everyone would protect their own rights. They would not compete or grow jealous of one another. They would collectively defend and implement each other's rights. Thus, Locke implies that humans' pathway to power is collaboration and cooperation, where everyone enjoys equitable status.

In each state of nature, a pattern emerges that people are driven by self-preservation. Humans grab power to secure their physical and emotional needs. However, each human type takes a diverging path to secure itself. In Hobbes' state of nature, people snatch from others so they can gain an upper hand over others. They compete with one another until their existence is ensured. In Rousseau's state of nature, people are jealous but compassionate too. They do not snatch from others but resort to compromise. They force a stalemate where everyone is contented. In Locke's state of nature, people collaborate with each other. They are neither afraid nor jealous but live cordially with each other. They cooperate on natural rights to ensure a peaceful habitat.

Based on this, we can deduce that competition, compromise and collaboration are three pathways of power. In competition, the win comes at the expense of the other's loss. In compromise, a small loss gives way to a higher return later, while in collaboration, all parties win. However, these pathways are developed based on the human types put forward by Hobbes, Rousseau and Locke. These types are based on the fallacy of an 'Ideal Type' as popularized by Max Weber. They do not depict the entirety of humanity but put in place broad categories of people. We may be tempted to disagree with all or believe that one of them is reality, but the truth is that the world has seen all these types manifesting in some shape. Another criticism of using this method to develop pathways is that the modalities of each state of nature are different. We cannot develop pathways when the baseline is changing. So, to satisfy these criticisms, let us relook at the hypothetical example from Chapter 5 where there are 50 labourers and one landowner. We established that the landowner had a need value in her favour. She had one of the three options to exercise the delta in need values. She could have used her power to get extra

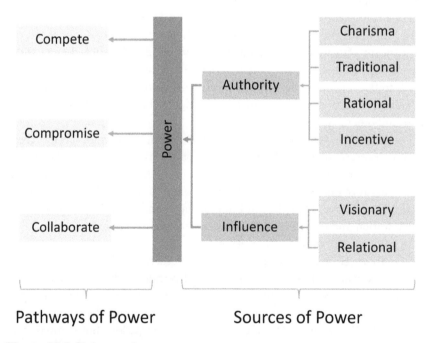

Figure 10.1 Pathways of power.

hours of labour, or she could let go of any privilege to generate goodwill or she might not even observe the need value. If she takes the first route, then she is using a competitive pathway as she is winning a reward for no cost to her while labourers are losing their labour hours for free. If she takes the second route, she uses a compromising pathway to power. She has compromised on her short-term gain by locking long-term influence over labourers. This influence can be used later. If she takes the third route, she is simply collaborating with labourers, bartering resources without looking at intangible benefits.

Another simple way of understanding these pathways is by taking the example of a pizza cut into six equal slices. You paid for the pizza, but your friend is also hungry and desires to eat the pizza with you. If you deploy competition, you will not share anything with him and eat all six slices yourself. In an act of compromise, you may lay your fingers on perhaps four slices and leave two for your friend. In cooperation, though, you and your friend get to have three slices each, where it does not matter who paid for the pizza or who has power. So, competition, compromise and collaboration remain three pathways of power even when we look at different case studies. Different actions depict different pathways in each case study. The intensity of actions reduces as one steps down the ladder from competition to compromise to collaboration.

It is pertinent to mention here that compromise is often confused with pragmatism. In pragmatism, people ditch their independence to fulfil their needs. They do not show any ideology, but in compromise, people maintain their freedom while enduring a short-term loss. They remain true to their goals and beliefs while sacrificing a small gain. A Sage can display compromise but not pragmatism. On the other hand, a Prince is full of pragmatism.

Chapter 11

STRATEGIZING THE PATHWAYS

It (power) is the name that one attributes to a complex strategical situation in a particular society.

Michel Foucault

As per Greek mythology, one day, Zeus was distributing gifts among Gods. Prometheus was also there among the recipients. Prometheus had created humans by then and wished a gift for humanity as well. However, Zeus spared no gift for humans. This did not go well with Prometheus, who stole fire from Hephaestus and gifted it to humanity. When Zeus came to know about the robbery, he became furious. He sentenced Prometheus to eternal torture by chaining him to a rock where an eagle would nip Prometheus' liver every day. Overnight, Prometheus's liver would regrow, only to be eaten by the eagle the next day. This torment repeated itself for thirty years until Prometheus was rescued by Heracles. When we investigate this tale, we observe that Zeus used his power in an act of competition, where he used power to punish Prometheus. But Prometheus used his power in an act of collaboration where he wished the same things for humanity as Gods. Looking at this mythology, can we deduce the underlying strategy adopted while using different pathways to power? What strategy is adopted in each pathway, and what does it mean for the opposition?

When we investigate any power trajectory, we see one of the three underlying pathways – Competition, Compromise and Collaboration. These pathways depend on the person harnessing power. These routes also have an inherent strategy embedded in them, indicating the power wielder's intention for the opposition. Recall that power is required when we are in a conflict. So, when we undertake any pathway, we showcase how we intend to deal with our counterpart.

To have a vantage point to understand this, we can map these pathways exercised by a few professionals before we deep dive into different strategies. Military generals and sportsmen mostly deploy competition as their pathway. When they do so, they intend to eliminate their opposition altogether. They work on a winner-takes-all or zero-sum strategy where one party emerges victorious while the other party loses. Investors and bureaucrats are proficient in playing the long game. They endure short-term losses to win big later. They display a compromising pathway, paving the way for the volunteer's dilemma strategy. They believe that a short-term loss is necessary to emerge victorious later. Traders and economists mostly deploy collaboration in their dealings. They try to maximize resources for everyone by generating connectivity between different areas. This allows them to generate a gain for everyone. Their de facto pathway becomes a win–win strategy for all. So, each pathway leads to a different strategy, and its outcome is different for the opposition.

To further explain these strategies, instead of giving real-life examples, we will investigate different creation mythologies propagated by religions and cultures. These mythologies will depict what pathway and its underlying strategy was deployed while creating the (wo)mankind. The result of all these creation myths is first human. Coincidentally, there is a consistency in every mythology that the first power structure predates the first human society, counter to evolutionary and anthropological evidence. There is a collective understanding that power came into being after the creation of societies, but all mythologies propagate that power is not a man-made phenomenon but something we inherited along with our creation. We were exposed to the concept of power at the time of creation, much before the advent of society. It is an agreed criticism that mythology is not a perfect way to look at the genesis of power in human development, though it gives us crucial insights into assessing the strategies deployed in power games.

All creation mythologies follow the rule of three as opined by Christopher Booker while investigating the plot of each story. In all mythologies, God, humans and evil forces make up the three characters of the plot. These mythologies revolve around the need to overcome the forces of evil. However, they differ in the positioning of the first humans in the plot. First humans positioning varies from protagonist to deuteragonist to secondary support. Based on this, we can broadly segregate the mythologies on what character the first humans presumed. We will assess how humans deploy varying strategies to win the power contest. In the first set of mythologies, humans were created as the main protagonist to actively compete against the forces of evil and chaos. They are actively trying to eliminate evil forces. The second set of mythologies discusses humans as deuteragonists after God defeated evil. The humans were to use power in a compromise to defend themselves if evil resurfaces. In the third group of mythologies, humans were created as secondary characters to subordinate God. They were to collaborate so Gods could focus on fighting off evil. Now let us look at some creation mythologies to make this distinction clearer.

Zero-Sum Strategy

In Abrahamic mythology, God created Adam as a supreme being to rule the planet. This was against the wishes of Satan, who believed that Adam was inferior to him and had no right to power. When asked by God to bow down to Adam, Satan disobeyed, for which he was banished from the heavens. Satan then waged war against humans out of jealousy which continues to this day. Satan intends to make Adam an evil being to prove to God that human creation was a mistake. However, Adam fears becoming evil, so he competes against satanic advances to stop the infiltration of evil in him. The kids of Adam are now in a zero-sum game where either they win or Satan wins.

In Uganda, the Buganda creation mythology follows the myth of Kintu, the first human. He was roaming on Earth when he met Ggulu (Sky God). Ggulu was impressed by the intelligence of Kintu and gifted his daughter, Nambi, to him. The couple dwelled in Magongo when they were joined by Nambi's brother – Walumbe (Disease God). Nambi and Kintu were blessed with many kids who formed the human race. Walumbe requested to adopt one of their kids. However, his request was denied, which made him furious. He started killing the kids. The couple then sought help from Ggulu, who sent Kaikuzi (Digging God) to fight off Walumbe. However, Kaikuzi was unsuccessful in capturing Walumbe as he dug a hole in Earth and has been hiding there till today. The earthquakes are brought down by the movements of Walumbe underneath the Earth. Humanity is on a constant lookout for Walumbe as he has been inflicting sickness and misery upon the kids of Kintu. A constant elimination race is ensuing between humanity and the chaotic forces of Walumbe.

In Siberian Tungusic mythology, Buga (creation God) created the world and all its elements. He then descended to his new creation, where he stumbled upon Buninka (devil). Buninka was unhappy with the creation of the world and bragged about his creation powers. The furious Buga challenged Buninka to create a strong enough tree to withstand the forces of the sea. Both created a tree, but Buga's tree was sturdy enough to withstand the sea while Buninka's tree swayed. Buga then began to convert Buninka into iron. However, Buga set Buninka free when he pleaded for mercy. Later, Buga created the first humans out of the elements of the world. However, Buninka wanted some humans for him as well. Buga allowed Buninka to keep all devilish humans and kept all virtuous humans for himself. Thus, a contest is ensuing in the world where virtuous humans of Buga are competing against devilish forces of Buninka to conclude who is superior.

Volunteer's Dilemma Strategy

In Chinese mythology, the creation mythology follows the tale of Pan Gu. There was chaos around, so he brought order to the world one day. He lifted the sky and pushed down the Earth to separate the two agents of chaos. These two parts made Yin (the Earth) and Yang (sky). Yinyang also forms the central theme of the Chinese philosophy of dualism. Pan Gu kept the two chaotic forces apart by acting as a separator between them. When Pan Gu died, his body parts became unique features of the world, like animals, mountains, oceans and sand, while his soul became the human race. The humans were then tasked to maintain order in the world. They are supposed to work towards keeping chaos at bay like Pan Gu to achieve the greater purpose of worldly peace.

Hindu mythology is circular, with each creation and destruction followed by the resting phase. This cycle forms one day in the life of Lord Brahma. The humanity in each cycle is instigated by Manu, the title of the first human in each cycle. The Hindu mythology is in its seventh cycle, where the name of Manu is Vaivasvata. Matsya Purana reveals that Vaivasvata was saved by Lord Vishnu (preserver of the universe) from the destruction of the flood brought down by Lord Shiva (destroyer of the universe). During this, Vaivasvata was exposed to the power of two lords. There is a consistency in each cycle of Hindu mythology to direct Manu to bow down to this cycle of creation and destruction. He is to compromise to this phenomenon and function as an agent to re-instigate humanity.

The Vietnamese creation mythology revolves around Au Co. She was a beautiful young fairy who was compassionate and sympathetic. One day, while attending to the sick, she met a monster who scared her. She converted into a crane and flew away from the monster. A nearby sea dragon, Quan the Am, saw this and killed the monster. Au Co was impressed by Quan the Am and they started living together. Later, Au Co bore a hundred humans, which started the Vietnamese civilization. However, Au Co and Quan the Am could not live together for long because of their diverging views. So, they split away, each taking fifty children with them. However, they did not stop loving each other. This is a metaphor for Vietnamese diversity; they should also love each other even if they are poles apart. They are supposed to compromise with the diversity of Vietnam to maintain order and peace.

Some other religions, like Sikhism, Jainism and Buddhism, have no creation mythologies. But they also believe that humans are created to maintain the balance on Earth. They are supposed to compromise rather than compete. It is this compromise that brings peace to their life. Hence, humans are to function as custodians of Earth rather than fight with each other.

Win–Win Strategy

The ancient Mayans believed that humans were created as a subordinate to Gods. This is depicted in the book of Popol Vuh. Before the world was created, it was inhabited by two Gods – Tepeu (maker) and Gucumatz (spirit). They created humans to honour them. Their first attempt to create beings from the mud was futile as mud beings crumbled in water. The Gods then created life from wood as it was sturdier. However, the created wood beings had no minds and hearts, so they could not worship Gods and created chaos. The unhappy Gods then wiped out wood beings, but some escaped to the jungle and lived as monkeys. The third attempt of Gods from maize resulted in human beings. The humans' first action was to worship Gods, which pleased Tepeu and Gucumatz. Thus, humanity is to worship and please Gods as they maintain the order of the world.

A look at the cultural mythology of Australian Aboriginals reveals that power predates the creation of societies. They believe in a period known as dreamtime when spirits roamed the planet. During this period, the spirits created all the features of the world and left Jiva (soul) and Guruwari (energy) seeds which created the first human. Spirits then told the humans about sacred sites. Humans, thus, have to please spirits by going to these sacred sites while spirits run the affairs of the world.

In Norse mythology, the universe is divided into nine realms. Between the Muspelheim (fire) and Niflheim (ice) realms, Ymir (giant) and Audhumla (cow) rose. Audhumla created the first human couple – Ask (male) and Embla (female). Odin then killed Ymir, created the world from his body parts and gave consciousness to the first humans. The first human beings were dwelling in Midgard to honour Gods in return for Gods protecting humans from evils. However, after the events of Ragnarök, many prominent Gods such as Odin, Thor and Loki died. The world was then devastated by natural disasters and floods. Two humans, Lifthrasir (male) and Lif (female), survived the destruction and re-instigated humanity.

Similarly, the ancient Babylonians believed that lord Marduk created the first humans to cooperate among themselves and honour him. The Babylonians believed that the universe was inhabited by Apsu (God) and Tiamet (Goddess). Apsu was unhappy with his kids and decided to kill them, but instead was killed by his elder son Enki. This enraged Tiamet, who waged war to avenge Apsu's murder. Enki's son, Marduk, was able to defend against Taimet's forces and killed her. The tears from the eyes of the dead Tiamet gave rise to the rivers of Tigris and Euphrates, which started the Babylonian civilization. Marduk then created the first humans to respect lords, so lords focused on protecting humans against forces of chaos.

When we dissect all these creation mythologies, we see three underlying strategies depending on the pathway adopted. In the first set, humans actively compete against evil forces. They try to eliminate the agents of chaos and destruction. If they fail, then evil will devour them in a zero-sum game. In the second set of mythologies, humans do not compete against evil but instead resort to compromise. They try to maintain the status quo of the world, which allows them to reap a bigger benefit of worldly peace. They deploy the volunteer's dilemma where a short compromise, not to pursue an elimination race, ensures harmony. In the third set of mythologies, humans are subservient to Gods. They cooperate with each other and the Gods. They do not participate in a duel against any destructive forces but leave it to the Gods to fight off evil. In return, they get peace and protection from God in a win–win situation for humanity.

The above-mentioned strategies also overlap with the three social contracts discussed in Chapter 2. Recall that custodians of a social contract enjoy great power. Their underlying pathway to exercise power nudges them to devise a social contract reminiscent of the three types of strategies they undertake to curtail their subject's freedom. In a singular social contract, a zero-sum game

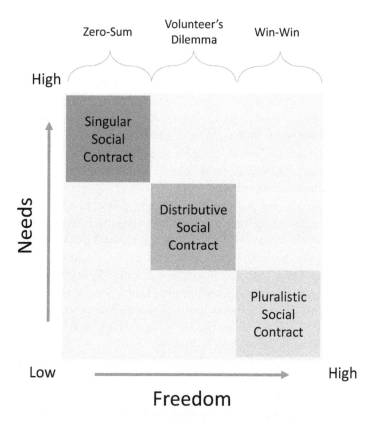

Figure 11.1 Power strategies mapped with a social contract.

is on display, where a strong central body makes and implements rules. The limits of freedom are greatly curtailed in this case. Anyone transgressing the limits of freedom can be eliminated through severe punishment. In a distributive social contract, a volunteer's dilemma is made by developing rules agreeable to all members of the society in an act of mutual compromise. In a pluralistic social contract, cooperation is the common denominator between members of the society. Collaboration ensures a win–win situation where no one has to trade their freedom beyond a certain limit.

Chapter 12

POWER GAME THEORY

Competition has been shown to be useful up to a certain point and no further, but cooperation, which is the thing we must strive for today, begins where competition leaves off.

Franklin D. Roosevelt

Before the commencement of World War 2, Adolf Hitler wanted to conquer Eastern Europe as part of the expansionist policy of 'Lebensraum'. He wanted to ethnically cleanse the area. This was driven by his ideology to implement ultra-German nationalism, the central theme of his rise to power. When he invaded Sudetenland in 1938, he made his intentions clear that he was deploying a zero-sum strategy. His conquests would come at the expense of subjugating inhabitants of Sudetenland. The other military powers of that era, the UK and France, rushed to stop him but later conceded to Hitler's designs. This resulted in the Munich Agreement. The agreement happened despite the military cooperation agreement between France and Czechoslovakia. The agreement is mostly seen as the beginning of the appeasement policy adopted by Neville Chamberlain and Edouard Daladier. They deployed a volunteer's dilemma strategy where an initial compromise would pave the way for European peace. It would halt the impending world war. Looking at the situation of 1938 from a game theory perspective, Hitler used competition while Chamberlain adopted compromise. However, the appeasement turned out to be futile as the UK was thrust into the war. They initially defended themselves, then halted German assault and later dismantled the Nazi regime. Had the UK not done so, Nazi Germany would have continued its march eastwards and westwards. So, what led the UK to change its strategy from volunteer's dilemma to zero-sum? Can we develop a game theory based on this example? Do we know how actions of the Sage trigger reactions of the Prince when playing the game of power?

Earlier, we established that there are three pathways to power. Each leads to a different underlying strategy. These strategies are not mutually exclusive but broad categories that help us distinguish what the power wielder intends to achieve. In reality, people mix these strategies as the situation evolves. Each strategy has its own dynamics, and its results are different.

The de facto pathway of the Prince is usually competition and hence zero-sum strategy. Niccolo Machiavelli has preached annihilating the adversary so that no one contests the power of Prince. However, Prince is pragmatic enough to use all three pathways as is needed to ensure its survival. On the other hand, the Sage is also fully capable to deploy any strategy which results in the implementation of the ideology. Despite the Prince's flexibility, we notice that the game theory depends on the Sage's starting position. It is because the Prince holds the power structure and the Sage is threatening the structure with a new ideology. If the Sage intends to use competition as the pathway, then the society is embroiled in a zero-sum game despite the Prince intending to use a different pathway. Similarly, if the Sage intends to deploy compromise, then that is only possible if the Prince is also willing to compromise or cooperate. Win–win happens when both the Prince and the Sage agree to collaborate. The Sage's intention to achieve a given level of independence determines the pathway. This can be analysed from the game theory chart below on how a Sage's pathway forces a strategy on the Prince.

Let us explain the game theory matrix in more detail by revisiting the hypothetical example of eating the apple from Chapter 2. Our need to eat the apple directly conflicts with another person's need. That person either wanted to have the apple for themselves or wanted to stop us from eating it altogether.

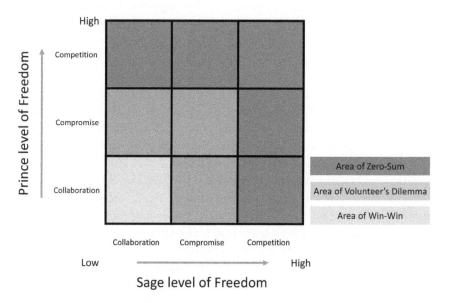

Figure 12.1 Power game theory matrix.

Our need directly conflicts with another person's need. Let us assume that we want to have the full ownership of the apple. We do not intend to share it. In this scenario, we are displaying a higher level of independence. We want to have uncontested ownership of the apple. This implies that our pathway is competition, where we intend to completely fulfil our need while the other person does not get anything. Notice when that happens, then, despite the other person's pathway to share the apple or propose another solution, the contest becomes a zero-sum game. So, whoever starts with a higher position to exercise independence dictates the underlying strategy. Hence, power game theory implies an escalation advantage but not a first-mover advantage. The person who escalates first forces the other to a given strategy. The escalation advantage, though, does not entail who wins or loses. The winner is decided by who invokes more power in the applicable situation.

When we look at events leading to World War 2, we get evidence of this. Germans pursued a competitive pathway where they wanted to dominate the whole of Europe. They had shown their intention, which was to throw all of Europe into a zero-sum game. On the other hand, the UK, with its appeasement policies, was pursuing compromise. They intended to use Czechoslovakia as a volunteer to ensure peace. However, this bait did not budge Germans. Germans attacked and controlled most of Europe, where their expansion reached the doorsteps of the UK. Had the UK kept on pursuing the volunteer's dilemma by ceding more control to Germans, they could have been annihilated as it was evident that there would be one winner of the war. This forced the UK into a full-blown war where they, too, pursued the elimination of Hitler. The initial phase was rocky, but the UK, helped by the Soviets, French and Americans, invoked more power. When this happened, the Allied troops prevailed and dethroned Hitler in this contest of zero-sum. So, we see that Germany's pursuit of competition forced the UK to enter into a zero-sum game which ended in Hitler's suicide. This is also validated by the above power game theory matrix.

While these war strategies were unfolding between the UK and Germany, there was another set of strategies being deployed between Italy and Germany. One may be nudged to believe that there was cooperation and win–win strategy, but the reality is that it was a volunteer's dilemma territory. It was because Mussolini was using compromise while Hitler was pursuing collaboration. Hitler had limited plans for Africa. He wanted to concentrate on Europe, while Mussolini wanted to erect an empire in Africa. Mussolini agreed to support Hitler in Europe in return for Germany supporting Italy elsewhere. So, despite Hitler's pursuit of cooperation, he had to resort to a compromise. It became a volunteer's dilemma where Hitler had to throw his troops into North African theatre. He had to over-stretch his defence line to support Italy. This strategy backfired and became one of the reasons for the downfall of Nazi Germany.

Another way to validate the game theory matrix is to do a thought experiment. Imagine you and your friend are on an adventurous desert drive when your car breaks down. There is no communication method to seek rescue. All you are left with is a water bottle. You did not notice any human population or oasis while reaching the deserted spot. To survive, you must walk back for five days. There is scorching heat with tough desert terrain ahead of you, and the only way to remain hydrated is with one water bottle. Both you and your friend are certain of death without that water. The need value of water goes exponentially high for both you and your friend in a span of few minutes. What will you do? Will you pursue competition where the goal is to have that bottle completely? Or will you pursue compromise where the goal is to let go of water for a while and settle on something big later? Or will you cooperate with your friend, where the idea is to share the water? Each pathway means something for your friend. Let us say that you also have a gun, so you know you have more power than your friend. You can materialize your need as you can invoke more power. In this scenario, will you pursue cooperation where you have half a chance to live? Both you and your friend may die in that case. If you take a compromising pathway, you may settle on a mechanism to drink the water, depending on who dies first. In that situation, you may die first and then your friend gets to have the water. But if you take the competition pathway, then your life is secure. But by doing this, you are effectively signing the death warrant of your friend. Once you show your intention of owning the water completely, your friend will be forced to retaliate irrespective of the pathway he wanted to adopt. Perhaps, the friend wanted to pursue cooperation or compromise. But because you pursued competition, your friend is forced in a zero-sum game. He also knows that death is certain without the water. So, your friend will also be forced to fight it out with you as chances for him to live are bleak irrespective.

Looking back at the game theory, we see a greater probability of zero-sum prevailing over win–win in the game of power. It is because anyone pursuing a competitive nature forces a winner-takes-all territory. The prevalence of zero-sum strategy is five times likelier than a win–win situation. In five out of nine possible scenarios in the power game theory matrix, zero-sum prevails. We can also observe this intuitively around us where we see more power struggles than cooperation. The whole school of realism is built on the same premise that accumulating power and pinning the adversary is a justified evil; otherwise, anyone can thwart the Prince and escalate the situation. However, realists completely discount that accumulation of power is already considered a competitive pathway. The Prince unintentionally escalates the pathway which results in a zero-sum game where each competitive action by a Prince is answered by more accumulation of power by its adversary. It becomes a never-ending race for the accumulation of power. However, if the Prince remains within the ambits of cooperation and collaboration, then lasting peace can be ensured. The Sage can be accommodated by cooperation, and new ideologies can be allowed to flourish in society without triggering a race for power.

One may question whether escalation can be softened through the art of persuasion. The adversary may be persuaded to compromise or collaborate to avoid a zero-sum scenario. The answer is that it is indeed a possibility. Negotiation is one such mechanism to make the other person step down the escalation path. Negotiation is thus not the art of getting what one needs but of persuading the other to step down the pathway ladder. This is what the intention should be while negotiating any conflict. Whether these negotiations are business-related or geopolitical, negotiation should be gauged by looking at the starting and endpoint of the adversary. When the Munich conference occurred, Chamberlain and Daladier were too focused on ensuring peace. They were pursuing a compromise with Hitler so that he would take a lighter pathway. Instead, they unknowingly allowed Hitler pursue competition and have Sudetenland. They failed miserably to de-escalate the pathway ladder.

Part IV

POWER STRUGGLE

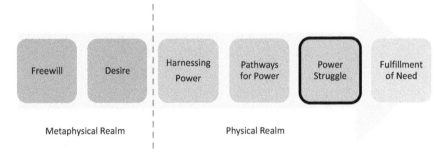

Figure IV.1 Zone of power struggle.

Chapter 13

DISTRIBUTION OF POWER

Politics means striving to share power or striving to influence the distribution of power, either among states or among groups within a state.

Max Weber

Pakistan became an independent country in 1947. There was civilian rule until 1958 when military rule took over. The junta continued their rule until Zulfiqar Ali Bhutto became the first democratically elected prime minister in 1973. However, Bhutto's initial brush with power did not come through democratic practices. He infiltrated the military cabinet of Ayub Khan as a civilian minister in 1963 and orchestrated his political rise from within the military circles. After the civil war of 1971, support for the junta dwindled, and under eventful circumstances, Bhutto proclaimed power as a civilian. He then put the then military chief – Yahya Khan – under house arrest and proceeded to sideline many senior military officials. He ensured that he faced no resistance from the military. He ruled Pakistan with an iron fist where he subdued any dissenting voice until he was deposed by his appointed military chief, Zia-ul-Haq, in 1977. Bhutto's sudden rise and fall give us a lesson that no power is eternal. When a new power sprouts, a section of the society helps it to reach the top, but another section of the society also emerges to fashion its downfall. Each section has power, but the distribution of power among these sections defines society. Based on this, can we develop a model to understand how power is distributed in society? Do elites control power, or have commoners wrestled control?

We know that power is sourced from authority and influence. Until the power does not become absolute, no one can claim to have all three dimensions of power. It is because power is distributed in the make-up of society. The power distribution in a system can vary from an individual to the general public. The spread of power is hypothesized by many philosophers. These theories broadly fall into two divergent schools of thought – elitist and pluralist. Though many of these theories explain government power, the underlying theme of these theories can be applied to a society as well.

Elite – The elitist view explains that power is concentrated in a handful of people in a society. Elites come from influential backgrounds which allows them to hold a pivotal position in society. Elites dominate the power circles where one elite is replaced by another elite. Many philosophers have put forward their version of elite theory based on their functional and conflictive views. More about functional and conflictive views is discussed in Chapter 14. The elite school of thought explains how power is monopolized among a few. Elitist philosophers believe that civilian rule is utopian, and democracy is a farce. However, elite theories differ on whether an elite rule is inevitable or not. Some theories focus on why elites gain power, while others focus on how elites stay in power. The Prince may or may not be an elite but for the purpose of this book, the word elite can be read in conjunction with Prince.

1. Varna: The first proponent of elitist school of thought were Hindus who believe that society is divided into four segments – Brahmins, Kshatriyas, Vaishyas and Shudras. Brahmins are born from the naval of Lord Brahma, the creator of the world. Kshatriyas from his hands, Vaishyas from his thighs and Shudras from his feet. Based on the body parts of Brahma, the power is distributed between Brahmins and Kshatriyas in society. . This theory pins the power elite as a static group where power is concentrated within a specific sect of people. It preaches that power is based on a birthright rather than skills or intellectual capability, so anyone born in the family forms the power elite. Many people believe that the 'Jati' system in India is an extension of Varna, but this system emerged much later and is a mere segregation of people according to their profession, such as Khatris (merchants), Lohars (ironsmith) and Gandhis (perfume makers). Varna can be explained in real life by noticing the power distribution in medieval Europe, where power cascaded down from one generation of royals to another. The main criticism to Varna is that it fails to explain how common people wrestle power from elites.

2. Vilfredo Pareto: Vilfredo Pareto's elitist theory believes that elites control power. He split the ruling elites into 'Lions' and 'Foxes'. He describes lions as those who rule with an iron fist and use decisiveness and dictatorial governance. However, they lack the intelligence or shrewdness to remain in power, so they induct foxes to make up for their weakness. Foxes is the word Pareto used to describe people who infiltrate power corridors through their cunningness and diplomatic manipulation. The term fox is also discussed widely by Niccolo Machiavelli in his political

theory. Foxes can be used to define the concept of Prince as well. Over time, foxes make up most of the power elites while lions are pushed to the brink. However, foxes lack the decisiveness of lions, and a minority of lions orchestrate a coup to take back power. So, power initially shifts from lions to foxes through the constant induction of foxes, and then a coup brings lions back to power. The power bounces between lions and foxes in a process called 'Circulation of elites'. It does not reach a common person. That is why he called history a 'Graveyard of Aristocracies'. Bhutto's rise to power is a good example of the Pareto theory. He assumed the role of a fox and infiltrated the military junta to become relevant in power corridors. He then managed to sideline the military and proclaim power. However, he was thrown out by the same junta he set aside a few years earlier. Though Pareto's theory explains a lot about elite capture, it fails to explain the process of revolutions and the democratization of nations.

3. Gaetano Mosca: Like Pareto, Mosca also believes that elite rule is inevitable even if there is democracy. He broadly segregated society into two – Rulers and Ruled. He believes that the ruling class is organized and skilful while the ruled class is unorganized. The ruling class occupies politics, military and finance, which keeps them as part of the ruling elite. Wealthy individuals, politicians and military generals organize themselves to keep a firm grip on power. This view contrasts with Pareto's view, where he believes that lions and foxes occupy power because of their decisiveness and cunningness. Mosca took a dim view of democracy, where he believes that even in a democracy, the ruling elite occupies positions that extend elite power. He did not believe that democracy is 'By the People'. He believes that elite rule is inevitable as even in democracies, elites can influence people to vote them into power. This theory also explains that elites can capture power even in a revolution. The rise of Abdul Fatah El-Sissi in Egypt explains this sequence of events. The Arab Spring dislodged the political power of Hosni Mubarak. After that, Mohamed Morsi came to power through democracy. However, El-Sissi was well positioned for a power grab as he controlled military power. He then led a coup d'état and brought back the same set of elites who worked under Mubarak. So, one elite in Mubarak was replaced by another elite in El-Sissi.

4. Robert Michels: Robert Michels put forward the 'Iron Law of Oligarchy', where he postulated that elite rule is inevitable. His theory was critical of huge bureaucratic societies and, in particular, democratic setups. He emphasized that the reason for their downfall is their size. Since decisions cannot be taken with an unorganized crowd, hence, people with

skills and specialization are required to understand different perspectives of the crowd. These specialist people become representatives of a section of the crowd. This leads to a hierarchy in the form of bureaucracy. Over time, the gap between leadership and the common (wo)man is widened by multiple layers of bureaucracy. This alienates people, and they become disillusioned. The power then falls into the hands of a selected few oligarchs who form bureaucracy. So, if bureaucracy happens, the structure is captured by oligarchs. Michels differs from both Pareto and Mosca in the sense that they believe that elite capture happens from the onset, while in the case of Michels, elite capture happens in multiple steps. Michels' theory can be explained by using the example of the USSR. The Bolshevik revolution kickstarted communism in the USSR. However, the Communist Party was so big that multiple layers of organization were needed. This led to a hierarchical structure in the Communist Party, which paved way for an oligarchy. Robert's theory can also be applied to corporations, which deploy a hierarchical structure. Many traditional industries, such as airline, steel and manufacturing, deploy a hierarchy of managers, distancing factory workers from leadership. This ultimately results in a conflict between labour unions and managers. The main criticism of Michels' theory is that elite capture is a threat rather than a law, as seen in many big organizations which deploy hierarchy and bureaucracy. However, they have an efficient decision-making process and deliver exceptional products such as Apple. Likewise, democracies can be big, but they can also be participative as with Switzerland where referendums are used widely for decision-making.

5. C. Wright Mills: Unlike other elite theories, C. W. Mills did not believe that elite rule is inevitable. Mills believes that elite rule is because of power resting in few institutions. He believes that power revolves around the government, military and corporations. He believes each institute has varying influence to exercise power based on societal needs. Where the economy takes the central stage, corporate CEOs become the elites. When the country is at war, military generals take the central stage, and politicians form the core of the elite when the federation is in danger. These three institutes form the core of elites. Mills called the US government 'Lieutenants of the Economic elite'. He also believes that the elites from one institute, like the military, can become elites of another, like the government. Since these elites come from similar social statuses and backgrounds, it helps to create mutual trust. He believes these elites garner unprecedented power without accountability by controlling mass media too. The media controlled by elites is, thus, used to brainwash the population to keep them quiet and passive. Mills further opined that

elites are self-recruited and usually come from privileged backgrounds or graduates from top schools. This theory explains the elite culture that prevails in the political space of Israel. It is almost customary in Israel for military personnel to become prime ministers and occupy political power due to the security situation prevailing in the country. The main criticism of this theory is that it focuses on the control and decision-making dimension of power without looking at the role of interest groups and social media not controlled by these three institutions.

6. Ian Budge, David McKay and David Marsh: Unlike Mills, this theory does not believe that elites come from specific institutions. Instead, they believe that power is captured by elites whose views are not necessarily aligned. These elites may form alliances with each other on some issues and may compete against each other on other issues. They called it the 'Fragmented elite' theory. They believe that it is impossible to have a monopoly over power by a specific group of elites. There is bound to be conflict among elites which leads to fragmentation. To understand this theory, we can look at the Indian elections of 1989. Congress Party and Janata Dal contested the elections. Both political parties had elites at the helm. Congress Party was led by Rajiv Gandhi, the fourth to lead Congress from the same family, while Janata Dal was led by Vishwanath Pratap Singh, who came from a family of rulers of Manikpur. Interestingly, Singh was a minister in Gandhi's cabinet formed after the 1984 elections. So, two elites in alliance in 1984 were competing for the political power of India in 1989, depicting fragmented elites.

Pluralist Theory – While elite theories talk about a selected few occupying a position of power, the pluralists believe that power is distributed among an array of people. Even if someone has no power, they may be represented through someone who has power. Pluralists believe that society takes back power from the elites if they continuously prioritize one section of people over others. Hence, elite rule is impossible for long as people quickly dismantle the hegemony of elites. The pluralist school is heavily geared towards democracy and republicanism. However, it does not advocate 'true pluralism' or communism of power. The pluralist school of thought concedes that a few people in society wield more power than others due to various elements such as wealth, status and knowledge. The pluralist school criticizes elite theories because elitists put a lot of emphasis on the control and decision-making dimension of power, paying no heed to the second and third dimensions of power. However, the pluralist theory is criticized for paying a lot of attention to shaping desires and opinion dimensions of power while downgrading the first dimension of power. Pluralists also fail to consider that elite capture is possible even in a pluralist society. For the purpose of the book, pluralist can also be read in connection with Sage as they are inherently common people who are driven by their ideology to better the society they live in.

1. Karl Marx: Marx gave a radical pluralist theory. He believes that society is split into Bourgeoisie and Proletariat. The bourgeoisie are small in population, but they make it up by having a higher share of power. They become elites of society by controlling the means of production. Proletariat, on the other hand, are the working class who make up the bulk of the society. He believes that the Bourgeoisie elites subdue the Proletariat and siphon benefits from them to their advantage. He believes that these two groups are in constant conflict with each other. A power struggle ensues, which results in revolutions and a classless society. Marx's pluralist view is that elitist hegemony on power inevitably ends in communism, where power is distributed among the public. Spring Revolutions of 1848 are good examples of Marx's theory.

2. Robert Dahl: The most influential pluralist theory was postulated by Dahl. He believes there is no specific group whose interests are consistently protected. Rather, he believes that when someone's interest is prioritized for long, an opposing section emerges to compete. The opposing group organizes itself and then lobbies to protect its own interests. That is why Dahl believes elite rule is theoretical. Though he believes power is not distributed evenly in society, the power differential does not skew favours towards few people. The rise of the Labour Party in the UK is an example of Dahl's theory, where labour union interests were not protected in the early part of the twentieth century by two leading political parties of that era – the Conservative Party and Liberal Party. This resulted in the formation of a political party, influenced by labour unions. The Labour Party later had a steady increase in popularity, where it toppled the Liberal Party to become the main opposition to the Conservative Party. Its manifesto was driven by the interests of labour unions.

3. J. J. Richardson and A. G. Jordan: Richardson and Jordan have put forward a more moderate version of the pluralist theory called 'pluralist elites'. They opined that elites represent interest groups, corporations and labour unions. Elites derive power from people and have varying influences to protect their association interests. Some groups are well represented than others. Those who are not well represented organize themselves to protect their own interests. In this way, each section of society is represented by an elite trying to influence the decision-makers in their favour. The decision-makers, thus, are merely there to reconcile and reach a compromise to not alienate any section of society. Many

parliamentary democracies in developing part of the world are examples of this theory, where an elected elite represents the interests of its constituency. The post-Brexit trade deal is an example to explain this theory. The leaders of both the UK and EU left out fishing as a compromise to finalize a trade deal. So, while other sectors of the country benefitted from the Brexit deal, the fishing industry was left out. It was natural for the fishing lobby to push the UK government for a new trade deal. This finally happened in late 2022 when a new trade deal was reached between EU and the UK. Though this theory explains many situations, it fails to explain why revolutions take place if common people are well represented by elites.

Through these theories, we understand different models of power distribution in a society. There are historical examples to explain each theory, but there are other examples where these theories fail to explain the power distribution. There are both proponents and opponents of each theory. Each school of thought explains a specific climate where the theory prevails. So, instead

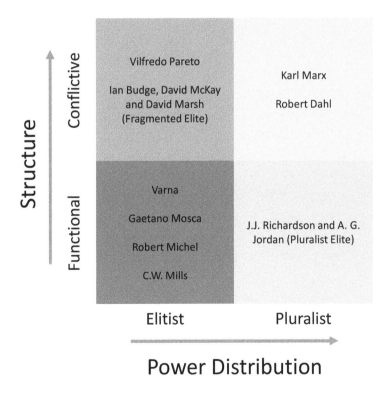

Figure 13.1 Elitist and pluralist models.

of applying these theories in isolation and backing one hypothesis, we need to look at these theories as a possible power distribution model. While the elitist school may believe that emergence of Sage in a society is a pipedream, Pluralists believe that a Sage can emerge to thwart elitism prevailing in the society.

Chapter 14

SOCIETAL BEHAVIOUR

People are dangerous. If they're able to involve themselves in issues that matter, they may change the distribution of power, to the detriment of those who are rich and privileged.

Noam Chomsky

Temujin was a Mongol leader who founded the largest Eurasian empire in the twelfth century. He came from a humble background but rose through the societal ranks to become a tribal chief. He then consolidated power by striking a network of alliances with other tribes and defeating any regional rivals. He successfully grouped all Mongol tribes under one flag and proclaimed himself as Genghis Khan. Even though he came from a background promoting tribalism, he rose above his prejudice and organized an army based on merit. He promoted many lowly ranked soldiers to senior leadership positions based on their performance. This made Mongols one of the most formidable armies in the world. As his empire grew, he ensured not to empower any tribal faction to the extent that could jeopardize his kingdom. After his death, his heirs took over the empire, but they were not blessed with the same level of intellect and intelligence. A civil war broke out between his heirs for succession. The Mongols that rallied under Genghis Khan for a while went back to their infighting, which systematically eroded the Mongol empire until it tore into four kingdoms – Yuan, Ilkhanate, Chagatai Khanate and Golden Hord. On either side of the life of Genghis Khan, Mongols conflicted with each other, which greatly affected their territorial expansion designs. The prevailing organizational behaviour in the Mongol empire swung like a pendulum. It started with a conflictive structure where tribal chiefs were embroiled in battles and skirmishes, it then moved to a functional oligarchy where Genghis Khan erected the Eurasian empire along with tribal chiefs before culminating in a conflictive system where Genghis' heirs were marred with infighting. So, what triggered those different behaviours in the Mongol empire? What are the various kinds of organizational structures in a power system? Can we decode societal behaviour based on this case study?

To understand organizational behaviour, we must understand the 'functional' and 'conflictive' views of society. These are two diverging schools of thought on how society works. Both of these systems manifest, so we must understand both before hypothesizing organizational behaviour in a power system.

Many functional philosophers, such as Emile Durkheim and Herbert Spencer, view society as a well-lubricated machine. Each part of the society serves the broader goal of achieving peace and harmony. Power plays an important part in maintaining the social equilibrium of such societies. The members of the system coordinate and work with each other to meet the needs of the people. But philosophers such as Karl Marx view society from a conflictive lens. They believe that members of society constantly conflict with each other to maximize their individual resources. These conflicts create friction where personal needs are prioritized over societal needs. The conflict culminates by either displacing the leader or disrupting the whole social order in the form of revolution. However, the commonality between both functional and conflictive perspectives of society is that both agree that power is a constant in a society. The functional philosophers view power as a source of harmony, while conflictive philosophers view power as a source of conflict. The functional systems view power as insurance to maintain the social order, while conflictive systems view power as a siphoning tool to extract resources from subjects.

To elaborate on this, let us take an example of two parallel societies. One conforms to the functional perspective, and the other conforms to conflictive ideas.

The functional society will have institutions catering to the people's needs. Each institute follows the same set of rules and guidelines to achieve equilibrium. There is a near-perfect social contract. In this society, schools are tasked to educate; hospitals are tasked to provide healthcare, and police are tasked to put violators behind bars. Each institute derives authority from the same set of rules and guidelines to cater to the needs of the people. No one tramples on anyone's rights, which keeps the system in equilibrium.

But the conflictive society is marred with those who want to overturn the system. The leader of the system transgresses on rules made to ensure the needs of the people. This gives way to the conversion of Slaves into Sages. Sages do not stop from tearing away the whole societal order to pave way for a new ideology. A functional system usually shifts into conflict when power is not used within the framework. Instead of providing for the needs of the people, it is used to increase one's share of resources. Imagine in the above example of a functional society, if teachers transgress their power and preach religion rather than educating in school, doctors trade organs rather than providing healthcare in hospitals and law enforcement professionals take bribery rather than policing society. All this would defuse the equilibrium where power trespasses on safety needs. Here, power becomes a source of conflict than harmony. The environment becomes hostile, which gives birth to Sages who challenge the misuse of power. To segregate a functional system from a conflictive one, we must gauge the number of Sages in society. The more Sages in the system, the more conflictive it is.

When the system becomes conflictive, the status of the system becomes transitional. It does not settle in one form but keeps on evolving until it becomes functional again or gets destroyed completely. Many ancient civilizations which could not revert to functional criteria met a tragic end. Indus civilization is a prime example of such a demise. It got uprooted rather than being pulled back to functional parameters. The Indus civilization thrived in its initial days on the back of massive resources available around the river Indus. It displayed functional characteristics with institutes catering to the needs of the people. However, when resources became scarce, power could not satisfy its inhabitant's needs. It pushed the civilization into a conflictive mode. Its citizens then migrated out of the region until Mohenjo Daro and Harappa became ruins. The end of such societies has been the subject of Joseph Tainter's hypothesis on 'Social Decay'. He postulated the demise of society through three models:

1. Dinosaur – The system is destroyed when resources deplete at an alarming rate. The Princes in this system are too accustomed to the status quo. Instead of looking at satisfying the needs of the people during a resource crunch, they are unable or unwilling to change their ways. This leads to decay to the extent that the entire system collapses. The Indus civilization qualifies as an example of such a collapse where the whole society was uprooted due to a lack of resources. The current climate change phenomenon is another dinosaur in the making where the world leaders have kept a blind eye. It is slowly eroding the world's resources. This can lead the whole human race towards the same tragic end as dinosaurs.

2. Runaway Train – This system collapses due to its inability to grow. It depends on a new pool of outside resources to satisfy people's growing needs. But a time comes when no new pool of resources is available. This leads to decay, and the entire system crumbles under its own weight. Vereenigde Oost-Indische Compagnie (VOC), or East India Company, is an example of a runaway train. VOC went bankrupt when it could not bring in new traded goods despite its heavy investments in Asian trade routes.

3. House of Cards – This system collapses because of its sheer size and complexity. The system becomes too big and complicated to sustain itself, which leads to fault lines emerging. This leads to a total decay of the system. Former Yugoslavia came into being after the Austro-Hungarian empire broke up. It consisted of several ethnical groups who toed their own line. The complex make-up of society grew the tensions until several smaller states split to form their own identity.

To develop an organizational behaviour, we will look at the underlying functional and conflictive views of the society and chalk them against the distribution model of power where elites and pluralists control the system.

The organizational behaviour revolves around four quadrants depending on who controls power and how its members respond. As long as the system remains bound within the functional domain where the slaves can get their needs, the system remains stable. However, if the system moves towards conflict, then the whole society becomes unstable, irrespective of whether there is pluralist reign.

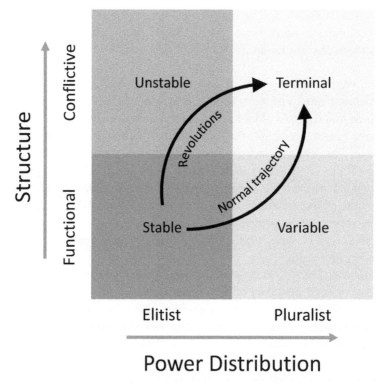

Figure 14.1 Societal behaviour.

The starting point in each system is an Elitist-Functional system. The system remains stable, where leaders are in control of Slaves. There are rare cases of Sages. One elite is replaced by another elite, and the system keeps on functioning. Elites are able to satisfy the needs of society. However, if conflicts emerge where a Sage challenges the elite with a new ideology to satisfy societal needs, then the system moves towards a Pluralistic-Functional quadrant. The system may remain functional, but due to pluralism, fault lines emerge where Sages stretch the boundaries of the system. These fault lines may not be significant enough to push the system towards anarchy. However, if the elite, instead of focusing on Slaves' needs, focuses on its own selfish agenda, then the system loses its credibility. It pushes the system towards conflict with elite trying to outmaneuvre the Sage rather than taking care of the Slaves. Even during the conflict, the system may exist, albeit with anarchy. At this stage, the system still has a last opportunity to move back towards functional parameters. If the elite ditches its selfish agenda and prioritizes people's needs, the system may crawl back to functional criteria. However, if the system reaches the Pluralist-Conflictive stage, where there is no end to the fighting, then that is usually the last stage before the entire system crumbles. Both elite and Sage ferociously stretch the system towards their direction until it is torn apart, and a new system emerges. The new system is led by either an elite or a Sage, depending on who won the duel. The system resets itself into an Elitist-Functional criteria before it also follows the same path of social decay.

An alternative path may be followed by some systems where instead of moving from Elitist-Functional to Pluralist-Functional, it moves towards the Elitist-Conflictive stage. Here, several Sages emerge in the system who pave the way for a revolution. If the elite can subdue the Sages, the system goes back to the functional spectrum, but if the elite cannot defend against the onslaught of Sages, a revolution takes place. From here, if a Sage replaces the elite, then the system gets reset. But if multiple Sages claim power after displacing the elite and infighting ensues, then the system is dragged towards Pluralistic-Conflictive view. In this situation, revolution is often followed by counterrevolutions until Sages stop contesting among themselves or new smaller systems are created under each Sage.

Each society goes through the same formation-destruction cycle. It is an unwritten prophecy for each system to crumble. The system either re-invents or crumbles. Samuel Huntington, in his famous book *Clash of Civilizations*, has identified several fault lines that trigger the crumbling of society. As long as elites satisfy the needs of the people and resist any Sages in the system, the system prevails. However, needs keep on evolving with the needs hierarchy until a time comes when needs can no longer be fulfilled. This is when the conflictive journey begins. The genius of the elite is thus gauged by estimating the delay it induces before a Sage emerges and the whole system gets decayed and heads towards a Pluralist-Conflictive quadrant.

Democracies are inherently Pluralist-Functional societies. They display fault lines on which political parties build their narratives. Most politicians pursue compromising pathways to power and do not exploit these fault lines to the extent of pushing the system towards the Pluralistic-Conflictive parameters. The genius of politicians is thus to keep the system functional despite the fault lines. Such societies thrive while celebrating their diversity. Hence, democracies are the most difficult forms of government as fault lines are knowingly sketched. However, when politicians pursue a competitive pathway, fault lines become obvious. These fault lines morph the system into the conflictive criteria, leading to the system's demise. Many power hungry politicians pursue this pathway. The most obvious evidence of this kind of behaviour was when Pakistan was heading towards electing its first democratic government in 1970. Sheikh Mujeeb-ur Rehman and Zulfiqar Ali Bhutto displayed a competitive pathway. Mujeeb had won the popular mandate while Bhutto was the second best. Both wanted to form the government but both did not budge from their positions, pushing the society towards the Pluralistic-Conflictive behaviour. The result was a full-blown civil war where East Pakistan became Bangladesh under Mujeeb while West Pakistan became Pakistan under Bhutto. Narendra Modi is currently displaying a similar competitive nature. India has several fault lines, including religion, ethnicity, language and culture. These fault lines appeared every now and then but were snubbed due to the genius of politicians at the helm. However, Modi, with his tunnel vision, is playing with fire by pronouncing these fault lines. India is still a Pluralist-Functional society; however, if the current trend continues, India might be pushed towards the Pluralistic-Conflictive mode. This may trigger an end to the colourful India we know today.

Now let's look back at the rise of Genghis Khan when he took power. The Mongols were already at the last stage of the system where the Pluralistic-Conflictive system was prevailing. Each tribe was fighting against the other to gather more resources. He constructed a new system where he defeated all rivals and rallied all Mongols under one emblem. He erected an Elitist-Functional system adhering to a modern-day oligarchical structure. Based on this organizational model, he expanded the empire massively, which allowed his kingdom to plunder resources from other regions. After his death, his heirs took centre stage, where the system moved towards the Pluralistic-Functional system. Multiple leaders who controlled a part of the kingdom emerged in the system. The functional element prevailed until the third generation of Genghis Khan. This was the time when new conquests became scarce. The influx of new resources dried up. Instead of prioritizing the needs of the system, each heir tried to siphon off resources from other parts of the kingdom. This triggered a bloody infighting which moved the system towards a Pluralistic-Conflictive quadrant. The system was then torn apart into four distinctive kingdoms, each with its own elite. This reset the journey of the Mongols into four Elitist-Functional systems.

The same organizational theory applies in the corporate world, where if shareholders, employees and customers are satisfied with their needs, the corporation flourishes. However, if employees or customers are disgruntled, then attrition starts. This starts getting reflected in the form of reduced tenure of employees and shrunk customer base. The leadership tries to induct new employees or explore new markets to compensate for the attrition. A constant uneasiness ensues due to the induction of new employees and new markets. Each employee and market come with its own needs. At this stage, corporations heavily invest in understanding employee and customer needs. If they can bring about a change, then the system moves back towards the Elitist-Functional quadrant, but if these investments do not yield anything, then the corporation tilts towards the Elitist-Conflictive quadrant. The leadership of these corporations then has a last chance to understand the needs of their customers. If they fail, then each customer stretches the corporation towards its agenda. The Pluralist-Conflictive stage is reached where leadership is toothless and each decision ends in a calamity. Such corporations go bankrupt or break away into smaller spin-offs.

In the case of GE, it flourished under Jack Welsh. GE became a household name and the most well-known brand. However, during his stewardship, he pioneered the 'Vitality Curve', which pitted one employee against the other. An uneasy competition ensued between employees and business units to outperform each other. Everyone wanted to maximize their results without looking at the overall corporation's needs. The system was consciously moved from Elitist-Functional to Elitist-Conflictive behaviour. Job security, which is an employee's basic need, was subordinated, and the best performers remained in the company. This was reflected in the attrition rate, where several employees either left the company or were laid off. The senior management bonuses were designed in such a way that each business unit was stretching the company in its own direction. Each unit wanted to maximize its own revenue without worrying about the outcomes of other business units. There was no single strategy to take the company forward, culminating in GE moving towards the Pluralistic-Conflictive mode. To top it off, there was little investment made in understanding the needs of employees, shareholders and customers. As this is usually the last stage in any system, even with extraordinary efforts to bring a functional system back to GE, it was too late. Divestments were made, and finally GE was split, each with its own organizational behaviour.

Chapter 15

STAGES OF SOCIETY

One cannot think well, love well, sleep well, if one has not dined well.
Virginia Woolf

Joseph Stalin was the editor of the communist newspaper *Pravda*. He raised funds for the Bolsheviks and rose through the ranks to become a leading figure in the October Revolution of 1917. After the death of Vladimir Lenin in 1924, he took control of the party and sidelined any contesting leaders such as Leon Trotsky. This helped him to consolidate power. He then instituted a great purge where he ordered to kill and imprison dissidents to weed out any opposition to his reign. Despite going through a shaky start to World War 2, where Nazis were knocking at the door, he inspired the Red Army to defend the country and then take Berlin as well. Considering his totalitarian regime, one may question how he stayed in power for three decades? How was he able to bind people in a system in a brutal environment? Why did the Soviets not topple him like they toppled his predecessor Nicolas Tsar? After all, both had a disastrous human rights record, but somehow Stalin stayed in power, but Tsar was ousted.

Power exists because we want to make rules, implement them and judge the violators of rules. The custodian of these rules maintains power. The rules are made to fulfil our needs. The influence of such power is restricted to those who get their needs fulfilled by the same set of rules. Power becomes a source of functional society and acts as a binder to keep the system together. Even the most heavy-handed power prevails if it caters to people's needs as was the case with Lee Kuan Yew handling of affairs in Singapore. However, if the rules are not universal but discriminatory, it leads to resentment. The hoard of people whose needs are not met in the discriminatory regime gives way to Sages who pull the system towards conflict. The Sages displace the complete system. The custodian of rules in this situation becomes a harbinger of a conflict. Even the most benevolent ruler may usher a conflictive system if it cannot impart protection to people's needs. So, despite the nature of power structure controlled by Prince or Sage, it can prevail as long as it caters to masses' requirements.

When the power is derived from influence, the system remains functional. People deposit their trust in the leader. The leader uses power derived from influence to hold a pivotal position in society. But when the power is derived from authority, especially incentive authority, then it gives way to some dissenting voices. These voices give way to fault lines which are the consequence of using authority over influence. In these systems, elites suck power to the top and unionize all three dimensions of power. They use their authority to take down Sages even before they can threaten the system. They use their power to forcefully keep the system functional. The more authority they use, the more fractured the system gets. If they keep neglecting people's needs, they unleash waves of Sages who ultimately overpower the elitist society and chop the system. Power becomes a race to the bottom in such societies.

Since power is sucked to the top in elitist systems, there is no hierarchy of power. So, when such regimes crumble, a huge power vacuum is created. The vacuum leads to a string of revolutions and counterrevolutions until the system becomes functional or is fractured into smaller units. But those elitists who use their authority to meet societal needs make themselves indispensable. They do not waste their power to forcefully keep the system functional; rather, they embark on developing sophisticated machinery which caters to people's needs. These elites embrace the physiological needs of the masses, which helps them to stay in power. However, they do not endeavour to fulfil people's psychological needs. They ensure that demands of people do not become psychological, where self-esteem gets reflected as resentment and freedom of expression. The genius of such elites is to tactfully manage physiological needs without allowing people to move towards psychological needs. This helps them to avoid anger and dissent. These elites become a source of binder for the system.

The striking difference between the two sets of elitist regimes, one which becomes a source of unbinding and one which binds people, is catering to people's needs. Those regimes crumble, which give no heed to people's needs as was the case with Idi Amin in Uganda. But elitist regimes that strike a balance in fulfilling people's needs and take down those who embark on fulfilling psychological needs prevail as was the case with Stalin. Depending on where the system needs lie, the chances of authoritative elitist regimes prevailing depend on where the subjects have progressed in their needs hierarchy. The chances of an authoritative elitist taking over any advanced economy such as Western Europe are slim not because of their strong democratic norms but because their subjects have progressed towards psychological needs. The industrial age helped their subjects to fulfil their physiological needs. Even if an elitist takes over such a system, a plethora of Sages will swamp the system to stop such a regime. In developing and underdeveloped worlds

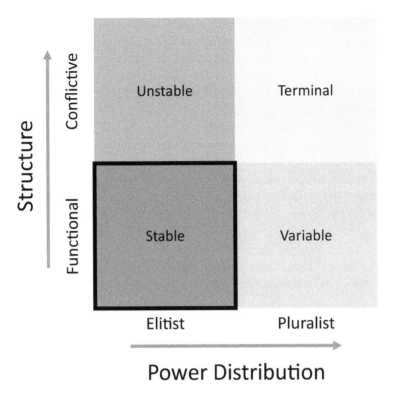

Figure 15.1 Elitist hegemony on power.

such as sub-Saharan Africa, where people are still reeling on basic needs, the chances of brutal and dictatorial elitist regimes prevailing are high. It is because people are still struggling to meet their physiological needs. Even the democratic processes in these countries have yielded authoritarians, as with Equatorial Guinea. Such regimes elongate their reign by embroiling people in their physiological needs while ensuring that any psychological need is met with a heavy hand.

In the case of Stalin, he kept the system functional throughout his reign. While he imparted physiological needs to people, he ensured that people do not progress towards psychological needs. Anyone progressing towards an advanced level of needs was purged.

The twin revolutions in 1917 had rocked the common citizen. The consequent civil war spanned until 1923, which made people fed up with the ensuing anarchy. So, when Stalin took over, people showed confidence in his ability to bring back peace. The initial public support helped him to solidify his position at the top. The famine of 1932 helped him further. He successfully inculcated fear in people's minds that they may be robbed of their basic dietary needs if he is removed. During the famine, he emerged as a defender of the people and waged war on the 'Kulaks' to showcase his concern for the general public. He portrayed Kulaks as enemies who are stealing and hoarding grain from people. In the guise of fighting the hoarders, he eliminated any dissenting voice to his reign. Similarly, during World War 2, he brought fear back to the masses that he is the one who could repel Hitler's attack. These crises gave him the impetus needed to stay in power while people believed that Stalin was focused on fulfilling their needs. A tiny minority, which lifted itself towards psychological needs, was purged. Contrast these actions to Nicolas Tsar. When Tsar was met with similar circumstances in the shape of the famine of 1892 and World War 1, his attitude towards managing these crises was not to posture himself as a saviour of the public. The 'Khodynka Tragedy' on the day of his coronation antagonized people. It gave the impression that he is not fussed about the plight of ordinary people and instead focused on a lavish royal life. This paved the way for Sages to initiate the revolution of 1905. When that failed, Sages hoarded themselves together in 1917, first in the form of Socialists and then Bolsheviks to topple the power structure. So, the mastery of Stalin was to derive power by fulfilling the physiological needs of the masses and creating a real or virtual enemy perceived as robbing people's needs. He positioned himself as the saviour of the people. These crises helped Stalin to gain influence too. If we look around history, we witness many long-lasting elites and tyrants using a similar template to remain in power. They focus on the physiological needs of people. Those elites who even fail to do this implode from within.

Many intellectuals believe democracy and plurality are the most important routes to a functional society. Other power modes in an elite society, such as monarchy or dictatorship, give heed to uneven distribution of resource, leading to resentment. However, as we have seen in the case of Stalin, it is not democracy but catering to people's needs which is the root cause of a functional system. If people are satisfied with their needs, elites prevail despite the form of governance.

To explain this concept further, let us take a hypothetical isolated human society reeling on the first level in the needs hierarchy. The only way to have food in this society is by gathering plants or hunting animals from the surroundings. An individual G has superior food-gathering skills through which he has collected more food than required. Society rallies around this person as he could gather more food for the society. He is meeting the physiological needs of the people. That person claims an elite position in society as predicted by Karl Marx theory which talks about elites controlling the means of production. If people remain satisfied with G's ability to gather and distribute food, then Varna's theory prevails where monarchy takes hold. G passes on skills to his next generation on how to cater to societal needs. By doing this, he can institutionalize power in the family. Many Gulf regimes display this sequence of events, where power is institutionalized within a family while society approves the monarchy as it caters to their needs. The consolidation of power by Stalin also falls under this sequence of events where society complied to Stalin's policies for almost three decades. However, if people are not satisfied with G's distribution mechanism, then he must induct a specialized person D to distribute food. So, power gets distributed between G and D, as hypothesized by Pareto. The society has two sets of elites, one for gathering food and the other for distribution. Power is institutionalized in these two people. From here, the timeline may diverge into 4 possible scenarios depending on the interaction between G and D and the needs of society.

1. G and D Are in Harmony to Keep Society Satisfied

Here, G can gather enough food while D can administer food distribution. Most of society is satisfied with their food requirements. Both G and D will recruit people of their own kind to solidify their power. This recruitment will lead to a hierarchy, which will kickstart bureaucracy. The society takes the elitist route as perpetrated by Michel where the top tier of power is occupied by G, followed by D. This sequence of events will eventually feed into oligarchies such as the one prevalent in China, where a single party rules while most Chinese are happy with their leadership.

2. G and D Wrangle, but Society Remains Satisfied

This case is reminiscent of fragmented elite theory. Here, G and D grow suspicious of each other. G downplays D while D perceives G as dispensable. In whatever case, a power struggle ensues between them. G fires D but since G cannot perform specialist tasks of D, he is forced to induct D1. However, looking at G's conduct, D1 grows suspicious of G and orchestrates the ouster of G. Since D1 lacks the capabilities of G, he inducts G1 to gather food supplies. However, the previous experience of both G1 and D1 does not allow cooperation and the wrangling goes on which leads to coups and countercoups. This is Pareto's sequence of events. As they wrestle, people remain satisfied with their needs as they are getting enough food supplies. As a result of continuous power struggle between G and D, they decide to project their skills to society. G lauds its food-gathering skills, while D chants its food distribution skills. They try to strengthen their hand by gaining influence among the masses. This situation complies with pluralist elite theory, where G and D project themselves to society as leaders to claim the throne. Both develop democratic tendencies even though they are elites. The practical example of this scenario is a two-party system of Bangladesh, where Sheikh Hasina leads the Awami League, daughter of Sheikh Mujeeb-ur-Rehman, and Khaleda Zia leads the Nationalist Party, spouse of former president Zia-ur Rehman. Both Hasina and Khaleda are elites who inherited power from their relatives. Interestingly, Zia fought under the vision of Mujeeb to liberate Bangladesh until Zia grabbed power after the assassination of Mujeeb. Both Hasina and Khaleda are now arch-rivals who lead two very divergent political philosophies in the democracy of Bangladesh.

3. G and D Are in Harmony, but Society Is Dissatisfied

In this scenario, G and D control food and its distribution, but people are unhappy. The food needs of society are not met while G and D collude and hoard resources. Here, the public may ditch the system altogether or choose a radical action by taking down both G and D and replacing them with another set of elites. In 1990s Pakistan, the political landscape was occupied by elites such as Benazir Bhutto and Nawaz Sharif. Benazir was the scion of the Bhutto political dynasty while Nawaz led a major business empire. Both conveniently ignored the plight of the common (wo)man. This resulted in both parties getting ousted in 1999 by a coup orchestrated by General Pervez Musharraf. Common Pakistanis celebrated the ouster of both parties, which paved the way for the military dictatorship in Pakistan for nine years.

4. G and D Wrangle and Society Is Dissatisfied

In this scenario, people are dissatisfied with their food requirements. If the food supply is a problem while G is enjoying a feast, people will demand G to gather more food. They will rally behind D to pressurize G. However, if the food supply is adequate and distribution is a problem due to D's incompetence, then people will rally against D and demand his ouster. In any case, people will support the group based on how they perceive the problem. This is an example of Robert Dahl's pluralist theory where people make decisions based on their interest. However, if both sets of elites are constantly wrangling with each other while ignoring the plight of people, then people will become disillusioned by both. In this sequence of events, people either ditch the system altogether or campaign to remove all sets of elites. This complies with Karl Marx's sequence of events. Spring Revolutions of 1848 are an example of such a sequence of events where the poor economic being of people led

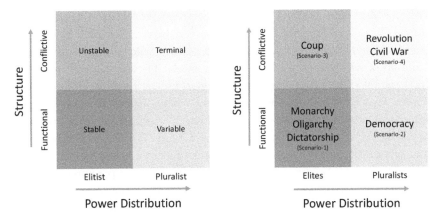

Figure 15.2 Shifting stages of society.

to dissent, and one after another, almost all Europeans rebelled against the incumbent power structure.

Notice that when the needs of subjects are fulfilled, the system remains functional irrespective of whether elites are tangled in a fight with each other or not. Society remains steady without drifting towards anarchy because the needs of people are being met. Elites fulfil people's needs but as soon as they drift away from their role, society gets pushed towards conflict.

Another observation from these four scenarios in elite rule is that democracy happens in Scenario 2. This happens when elites wrangle with each other while society is satisfied with the needs. Democracy does not prevail in any other circumstance. It is commonly understood that democracy is initiated by common people who are not satisfied with elite rule. However, when we analyse both scenarios where societal needs are unmet, revolutions and coups happen. When societal needs are not met, it becomes increasingly difficult to rationalize people's demands as anger and emotions take over. This pushes society into chaos and anarchy. When society reaches that tipping point, it becomes an unguided missile where revolutions and coups become the usual course of action. Revolutions usually do not usher democracy, as is the case with the Arab Spring, where protests brought another set of elites. Where coups happen, like in Pakistan, or make-shift democracy prevails, like in Equatorial Guinea, though, the system becomes functional, but it does not guarantee true democratic norms. So, the democratic tendencies in any society are initiated by elites under the compulsion of public needs. Elites usher democracy because they cannot reconcile their differences with other elites, so they go to the public to garner support. The best example to explain is the democratization of England. King John was embroiled in a bitter feud with rebel barons. When the king and barons could not settle their differences, the Magna Carta was signed in 1215. This enabled the creation of the first parliament in 1295 to bring accountability to the king's rule. The parliament was made up of wealthy and influential individuals. They were elites in society who controlled the power structure in England. Over time, the power of parliament evolved. The landmark event came when elites could not settle their differences among themselves in 17th century. The elites of that era projected themselves to the public to strengthen their hand. This led to democratization, where the public became participants in electing their representatives to the parliament. So, English democratization did not happen in one go but took centuries where we have the current system of elections.

To sum up, each society evolves. It usually starts with elitism. Once society grows, the needs of people evolve, which helps to form other sets of elites. If all elites conform to each other and protect people's interests, then power stays within a handful of elites. However, if disagreements emerge between elites, fragmentation occurs, eventually leading to a version of pluralism. The pluralism can range from organized democracy to chaotic revolutions. However, in each sequence of events, power's purpose remains catering to needs. Power becomes a source of binding the society as long as people's needs are protected. The unbinding of society happens when power ditches the very reason of its existence.

Chapter 16

TRAJECTORY OF SAGE

You only have power over people so long as you don't take everything away from them. But when you've robbed a man of everything, he's no longer in your power – he's free again.

Aleksandr Solzhenitsyn

Omar Al-Mukhtar was a resistance leader fighting against the foreign occupation of Italy in Libya. He was a teacher when Libya came under the occupation of Italy. He set aside his teaching career and became a guerilla fighter to fight the might of the Italian war machine. He led the struggle for the independence of Libya for 20 years. He was aware of his limitations as a fighter, so he did not attack Italians directly. Instead, he devised the art of hit and run, where he would lead a small contingent of soldiers to ambush Italian posts and then fade into the terrain. His tactics became an embarrassment for the occupiers. They first tried to pacify him and then negotiated with him. When their efforts failed, they put all their efforts to capture Al-Mukhtar. Once occupied, he was given a short trial by Italian courts and hanged on 16 September 1931. So, what led a teacher to become a guerilla fighter? How did a religious scholar turn into a war tactician to oppose the Italian occupation? How do ordinary people gather the courage to oppose power structures in any society and kickstart various stages of society?

To understand this, we must revisit the power matrix on how people fall into different classifications in a system. Humanity is divided into four groups based on their level of needs and independence. Each system is occupied by a Prince who controls the maximum power while the majority lives in the Slave category, who look upon the Prince for their needs. A few reside in a Sage group, pitted in a power struggle with the Prince.

The starting point of any ordinary person is Slavery. Most of humanity belongs to the Slave category anyways. Slaves do not downgrade their survival instinct. They are fearful of taking a leap of faith towards freedom. However, the day Slaves seek retaliation against anyone who tramples on their survival, they promote themselves towards a Sage group. They ditch their dependence and proclaim independence of their thoughts, actions and ideas. Many impactful leaders are defined by some event in their life, which makes them rebellious. That event forces them to lower their needs and wage a spirited fight against the Prince to fight for their independence. History is full of people who broke the shackles of Slavery and took on the trickery of Prince when their survival was threatened. Al-Mukhtar is an example of an individual who swore allegiance to the Senussi order. When Italians threatened Senussia, he left his teaching duties and became a resistance fighter. He shunned his survival instinct and became a Sage.

Once a Slave becomes a Sage, they either topple the Prince or get eliminated. The toppling of the Prince depends on whether the Sage can garner enough power. If they garner enough power, the Prince is displaced by the Sage. But if a Sage is unsuccessful, then they are eliminated by the Prince, as it is impossible to contain the actions of a Sage. In rare circumstances, when a Sage reprioritizes survival, they are pushed back to Slavery. So, the usual path to power for an individual is to start from Slavery and then dare to become a Sage. After becoming a Sage, they either harness enough power to topple the Prince or get eliminated. In case of Al-Mukhtar, he was aware that he did not have enough power to topple the Italians, so he devised guerrilla warfare. He wanted to inflict as much damage on Italian troops as possible so that occupiers are no more able to control Libya. Italians tried hard to persuade Al-Mukhtar to let go of his suicidal instincts to push him back into Slavery. They tried to seek a compromise, but since Al-Mukhtar was operating on a competitive pathway, the Italians had to resort to elimination by hanging. Notice that an ordinary life is a journey from Sage to Slave while a Sage's journey is opposite to normal life.

For the Princes, they are repeatedly tested by Sages. Ever since the dawn of human rights, pushing back Sages into Slavery has been the preferred method of a Prince. But historically, Princes have managed Sages by eliminating them. The Sages, anyways, are not optimist about life as their survival instinct is taken away, so eliminating them is the easiest way out for a Prince. However, if Princes are sceptical and suspicious, they confuse Slaves with Sages. They deploy the same practice of elimination on Slaves as well. Slaves remain subdued because of their survival instinct, but when suspicious Princes trespass upon their survival need, they entice Slaves to morph into Sages. This unleashes a revolution which is the consequence of the wrong tactics of the Prince. Revolution is converting many Slaves into Sages at the same time. While few Sages can be managed locally, managing a swathe of Sages simultaneously is tricky. So, revolutions are essentially a pile-up of Sages crafted at the same time. The Prince's failure to differentiate between tackling a Slave and a Sage has been the defining moment of many revolutions. The Arab

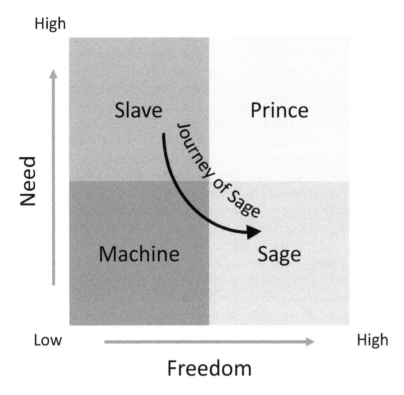

Figure 16.1 Journey of Sage.

Spring is a prime example where the Prince's mishandling of Slaves converted many into Sages. It took some time and regime change in a few Arab countries before Sages were pacified and pushed back into Slavery.

The fate of the incumbent Prince is decided by how much power they can harness. The system remains intact if they can derive more power than Sages. But if they cannot invoke enough power, then they are toppled. The Prince descends into Slavery. This shows the Prince's survival tendencies. It is evident from the stories of many kings and dictators who preferred exile than to stay in the society.

In 1931, Al-Mukhtar's suicidal instinct was insufficient to topple the Prince. He did not harness enough power to topple the power structure. However, eight decades after his death, many Sages successfully deposed a brutal regime in his country. Muammar Gaddafi had a dismal human rights record. The inhumane actions of Gaddafi were threatening the survival of many slaves. This converted many Libyans into Sages who waged assassination attempts at Gaddafi. Mass purging followed each failed attempt, allowing Gaddafi to continue his grip on power. Though he survived each assassination attempt, it triggered a downward spiral where each purging led to a greater conversion of Slaves. The conversion process was slow, so the aggregation of Sages did not happen, and revolution could not occur earlier. However, by 2011, the stacking of Sages was enough to trigger riots. The common citizens were fed up with the regime and were instigated by the events happening in neighbouring countries like Egypt and Tunisia. The Sages initially gathered in the cities of Bayda and Benghazi before engulfing Tripoli. The regime, to push back Sages into Slavery, announced heavy developmental spending. But this did little to thwart them. After Gaddafi failed to pacify Sages, he threatened them with extreme actions. However, once a Sage is crafted out of a belief, an idea or thinking, then it is difficult to subdue them. Gaddafi then famously stated that the food and drink of these people are spiked with hallucinogenic drugs because no sane mind would have challenged Gaddafi then. He vowed to fight like a warrior and die a martyr. After that announcement, massive waves of violence broke out throughout the country, where both sides cried foul play. Thousands of people were put in torture cells until NATO came to help. This drastically increased the power of Sages. At the same time, many government officials and generals defected, reducing Gaddafi's power grip. In the power match-up, Gaddafi lost, and his regime was deconstructed. He made a run for himself to ensure his survival but was ultimately killed in an inhumane way. The Sages won, and the Prince was toppled. Though no one has replaced Gaddafi's position in Libya yet, that is due to the underlying societal behaviour. The environment in Libya has moved swiftly from Elitist-Functional under Gaddafi to Pluralist-Conflictive with multiple warlords at the helm. The possible outcome is the creation of new autonomous or independent systems controlled by each fighting faction.

Similar events also manifested in Syria, where the incumbent Bashar Al Assad was pitted against hordes of Sages. The human rights record instigated the conversion of many Slaves into Sages at the same time. The Western forces allied with the Sages there too. When many government officials and military generals also defected, it was perceived that Bashar's power had drastically reduced. It was thought that it was a matter of time before the Libyan experiment would be replicated in Syria too. However, Bashar resurrected his power through his allies in Iran and Russia. At the same time, the division of Sages happened in Syria prematurely. While in Libya, Sages worked together initially and fractioned after toppling the Prince. In Syria, the Sages parted into different sects even before the deposition of the Prince happened. There was infighting within different factions. Sages' power was greatly divided while the Prince's power was increasing. The power equation was wrestled back by Bashar, which led to Sages caving. Many Sages were eliminated, and the rest were pushed back into Slavery as refugees. The survival instinct of Sages took over after years of fighting. This led to the 'European Migrant Crisis' in 2015, where many Syrians landed in Europe.

So, in order to become a Sage, one must lower their survival instinct, then embrace an ideology which seeks to impart needs to a society. On the back of an ideology and vision, gain influence in society and then vie to topple the Prince. Once the Sage steps into the power arena, the distribution of power in society kickstarts. It paves the way for varying societal behaviours (Chapter 14) and the different stages (Chapter 15) until the Prince is toppled. After that, the system needs to be brought back to functional parameters before anarchy sets in and a long transition period kickstarts.

Chapter 17

TRANSITION PERIOD

Our government teaches the whole people by its example. If the government becomes the lawbreaker, it breeds contempt for law; it invites every man to become a law unto himself; it invites anarchy.

Louis D. Brandeis

After the Balkan Wars, Albania declared independence from the Ottoman Empire. It aligned itself with the communist agenda. For most of the twentieth century, Albania remained under the influence of a command economy. After the declaration of the Fourth Albanian Republic in 1991, it moved towards a market economy. Along with other benefits of liberated markets came the nuisance of gluttony. Many pyramid schemes mushroomed across Albanian cities. These schemes were to function as a front end to launder money. Many politicians and celebrities endorsed them. People invested their life savings in these schemes, hoping to become rich overnight. By 1997, the size of these schemes became too big to add new layers to pay the old ones. The pyramid schemes fell with a bill exceeding a billion dollar. This triggered a crisis where people rioted on the streets. In the ensuing anarchy, there was thuggery, armed robberies and casualties until a change of guard happened at the top. The crisis lasted for more than eight months until a transition of power happened. So, is the transition of power always littered with anarchy as was the case with Albania? Or do we have a more civilized way to transfer power?

When power does not fulfil people's needs, the social contract breaks. The breaking of a social contract moves the system towards the transitory stage. People either migrate out of the system or turn violent. If people pursue an agitation path, then multiple factions dismantle the system. A power vacuum is created, which paves the way for anarchy. A mere presence of an individual at the helm at this stage is not enough. As soon as anarchy sets, stabilizing forces also emerge to fill the power vacuum. People look towards those who can guarantee basic needs. The transition period kicks in until the society is functional again. There are broadly two mechanisms through which a Prince is set aside. 'Throning' is when power is passed through an established mechanism to transfer power. 'Dethroning' is when no process is followed, rather, an ad hoc path is created to lead the society. Battles, civil wars, revolutions, civil disobedience and coups are all examples of dethroning. Dethroning is a controversial subject in philosophical circles. Some vehemently reject this process, while others endorse it.

Below are the views of some famous philosophers who do not endorse dethroning:

Socrates does not endorse dethroning as a transitional mechanism. He believes one should not break the social contract to oust the power structure. In Plato's *Phaedo*, Socrates argues that even if the government is unjust, one should still follow the laws and accept the consequences of disobedience. He believes that breaking the law can set a precedent for subverting the social order. He feels this practice is worse than enduring injustice. Instead, Socrates believes in working within the system to bring about change, even if it means suffering punishment or death.

Thomas Aquinas believes that subjects have a natural right to self-defence, but this right should be exercised with caution and restraint. He believes that people have a duty to obey the laws of their government if those laws are just and do not violate natural law. He believes that the use of violence, especially in the pursuit of overthrowing a power structure, is often motivated by selfishness or a desire for power. Hence, all dethroning mechanisms should be avoided as far as necessary.

Immanuel Kant puts a lot of emphasis on ethics and morality. In his book *Metaphysics of Morals*, he has highlighted that people have the right to complaints and grievances but not to active resistance or rebellion. He does not endorse the 'Doctrine of Necessity' to destabilize power structures. Kant argues that revolution is a last resort and that other, non-violent means of resolving conflicts and bringing about change should be tried first. He believes that using dethroning mechanisms is a sign of weakness or a failure to find more peaceful and rational solutions to a problem.

Daron Acemoglu and James Robinson argue in *Why Nations Fail* that dethroning is driven by economic and political factors. They believe that revolutions have both positive and negative consequences for society. However, political and institutional reforms are the best forms of toppling the system. The dethroning process should always be approached with caution. Great consideration should be given to the costs and risks involved.

On the other end of the spectrum are few philosophers who agree with the process of dethroning.

Henry David Thoreau took a mild view on dethroning. He authored an essay, 'On the Duty of Civil Disobedience'. He ditched the pragmatic approach of handling the dethroning process with caution. He criticizes doing a cost-benefit analysis while overthrowing the power structure. Rather, he advised everyone to rebel in a way that qualifies as just and fair. He believed disobeying the state as the right method to oust them. His inventive non-violent dethroning method was later cited by Mohandas Gandhi and Martin Luther King Jr's disobedience movement.

John Locke defends the right for dethroning. He believes that people are guaranteed natural rights. However, if these rights are violated and power structures fail to protect them, Sages reserve the right to revolt. He defends dethroning in *Two Treatises of Government*. However, he believes that the social contract should be followed as far as necessary. However, if the power structure continues the violation, then Sages may pursue dethroning.

Jean-Jacques Rousseau is another philosopher who supports revolution. He believes the power has an inherent duty to provide the general good. If they fail to do so, then dethroning is justified. He believes that if the power turns violent, subjects have the right to repel it with more forceful violence. His opinions are expressed in his famous book *Second Discourse*.

Karl Marx is the biggest endorser of dethroning. He believes that working-class exploitation can end if the capitalist class is overturned. He argues the upper class is never willing to give up the power. Hence, dethroning is a necessity to end the exploitation of the working class.

Based on these views, we might want to think that throning is a better way to topple the Prince as it comes without a hiccup. However, it varies from case to case. Anarchy has happened in many democratic transitions too, where a thorough throning process was followed. Many developing countries witness rigging allegations where the Prince fails to cede election results. There is no better spectacle of this than the 6 January 2021 Capitol attack in the United States when power was transitioned from Donald Trump to Joe Biden. Though the anarchy lasted a day, it could have easily engulfed the whole of the United States, had Trump not released a statement to stop the violence.

Still, there is a greater probability of anarchy settling in during the dethroning process. The reasons for extended period of anarchy in dethroning is because it is a two-step process. Initially (1) a Prince is taken down in an ad hoc process. The ad hoc process opens a window which allows multiple Sages to eye the lead position. So, in a second step, (2) competing factions fight to eye the leadership position until one emerges victorious.

The dethroning sequence of events was in full focus when we study Iranian Revolution. The first series of violence erupted to take down the Shah of Iran – Mohammad Reza Pahlavi – while the second series of violence were to take down Ruhollah Khomeini's rivals. Iran's revolution had both left- and right-wing elements. So, when the Shah escaped to the United States, the Khomeini group wrestled power from competing Marxist, socialist and secularists. Many of the Shah's loyalists later became part of Khomeini's group, which helped him to consolidate power and later persecute all competing factions. However, there is also a slim chance that no anarchy sets in when the dethroning process follows. Iraq went through an internal party coup where Saddam Hussein toppled Ahmed Hassan Al-Bakr in 1979, followed by the 'Baath Party Purge'. Anarchy did not happen as Saddam ensured that all his 21 potential rivals are taken down in one go. So, the transition of power was swift. While Khomeini took four years to consolidate power at the top, Saddam's rise to power happened over a few days. So, the same process of dethroning happened in two neighbouring countries at almost the same time, one ended up in four years of anarchy while the other one happened in a swift fashion with no anarchy.

The extended period of anarchy in dethroning sometimes is also due to the 'Thucydides Trap' concept introduced by Graham Ellison. Thucydides was a fifth- century BCE Athenian military general who believed that a war between Athens and Sparta was inevitable. He believed that it was because Spartans feared Athenians' growth. Based on this, Ellison hypothesized that a full-blown war is inevitable whenever a new power challenges the old power. As evidence to further his hypothesis, he looked at 16 historical power transitions. Out of that, 12 ended in a war. This may nudge us to believe that power transitions are inherently rocky when dethroning happens. Any new (Sage) power in a society is bound to invite a war-like retaliation from the old (Prince) power. But this is not necessarily the case as we have seen from the rise of Saddam in Iraq.

In the presence of conflicting philosophical views and historical evidence, it is not entirely possible to strike down dethroning as a mechanism. But before a Sage pursues this path, we need to determine the length of the transition period when Sage topples Prince.

Three main factors play a significant role in understanding how any transition unfolds. These factors are (a) the influence of the Prince, (b) the authority of the Prince and (c) the influence of the Sage. These factors help us to predict the transition period. These factors can be depicted through the legs of a triangle. The Prince's authority and influence make the triangle's base, and the Sage's influence makes the triangle's height. The area of the triangle predicts if the transition will be lengthy or short. The larger the area of the triangle, the greater the turmoil and vice versa. Recall that authority is hard power, and influence is soft power. So, the Prince always has the advantage of using hard power over the Sage. But the Sage has little-to-no hard power. Thus, the Sage can only invoke influence when the tussle starts in a society.

If the Prince has high authority and little influence as compared to the influence of the Sage, then the transition period is long. It is because the Sage exhausts all the influence to take down the authority of the Prince. This usually happens in authoritarian regimes where revolution is the de facto mode to topple the Prince. The dethroning mechanism is adopted, which triggers a prolonged period of instability. If we pick any revolution such as the first French Revolution of 1789, we see ordinary civilians dismantling the authority of the royal family.

In case the authority of the incumbent is low, but influence is high, while influence of the challenger is also high, then, that is usually the case when an interim setup has come, or a newly proclaimed power is in control. This scenario transpires in counterrevolutions or coups where a settled Prince has been sidelined and competing Sages with similar influence are vying for the top spot. The transition period in this case is longer as depicted by the area of the triangle. The events following the toppling of Nicolas Tsar in 1917 display this version of events where the competing factions were pitted against the Bolsheviks. Both enjoyed influence with little authority.

Where both authority and influence are low for the Prince while the Sage has high influence, then transition is small. This is part of all democratic transitions where an unpopular government is voted out. The Prince is left with little-to-no authority and has lost influence in the shape of a mandate. The transition is swift, which eases the new power into the role. This scenario also explains how Saddam swiftly transitioned into power. Al-Bakr had lost authority after his health deteriorated and he delegated the decision making

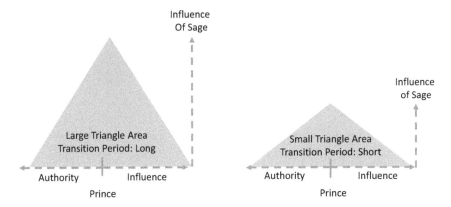

Figure 17.1 Model of transition period.

to Saddam. Later, he lost influence, also many Baath party officials defected to Saddam. But Saddam harnessed influence by changing the allegiance of party officials. So, at the time of transition, Saddam was pitted against little-to-no resistance. He walked straight into leadership with no hiccup.

There are other iterations of transitions but the likelihood of those scenarios is slim. Hence, they are not illustrated below (Figure 17.2).

Based on the above understanding of the transition period, let us look back at the case of Albania. We might be tempted to believe that the root cause of anarchy post-1997 was the fall of the pyramid schemes. People needed financial security which the government failed to provide. That may have triggered an anarchic period. To stem the anarchy, leadership was transitioned through a throning process of elections in June 1997. However, the transitioning period started a year earlier. There were elections held in May 1996 too with widespread rigging accusations. There were reports that the Democratic Party was intimidating opposition including the Socialist Party. Opposition parties withdrew from the second round of elections held in June 1996. The elections lost credibility, and the subsequent government did not have the mandate. It was merely fighting through authority. To make matters worse, the pyramid schemes fell after six months which eliminated any influence left with the government. This became a tipping point where dethroning was followed through a war-like situation. The Prince was fighting off the Sage through authority while the Sage had tremendous influence. The Sage had garnered this influence through giving a vision of financial security. The transition period in this case study followed the first iteration of transitions.

Prince Authority	Prince Influence	Sage Influence	Prevailing Regime	Transition Period
High	Low	High	Authoritarian	Long — Challenger / Incumbent
Low	High	High	Interim Setup	Long — Challenger / Incumbent
Low	Low	High	Unpopular	Short — Challenger / Incumbent

Figure 17.2 Transition period of regimes.

The transition period was rocky due to the authoritarian tendencies of the Prince. Here, the influence of the Sage dismantled the authority of the Prince while rival factions were subdued through subsequent elections.

To summarize, the transition period is not necessarily anarchic. It depends on the power garnered by Prince and Sage. In both throning and dethroning processes, an anarchic period can set in depending on who is able to invoke more authority and influence.

Chapter 18

GOAL OF TOPPLING THE PRINCE

Most powerful is he who has himself in his own power.

Lucius Annaeus Seneca

Alexander the Great was the king of Macedon. He succeeded his father in 336 BCE and embarked on a lengthy military campaign. His soldiers had an aura of invincibility where they successfully defeated one army after another. His empire stretched from Eastern Europe to South Asia. However, his most important conquest was that of the Achaemenid Persian Empire. He invaded the Achaemenid Persian Empire in 334 BCE. After a gruelling military assault, he conquered Persia. Though his de facto method to topple the empire was dethroning, he showed little competitive pathway. He integrated Persians into his empire and gave them equal status as Macedonians. He allowed many locals to keep their high-ranking status and allowed interfaith marriages. Based on this, can we understand what Alexander's goal was? We do know Sages are loaded with an ideology, but do we know what their goal is to topple the Prince?

Humans are driven by their needs. They support power structures that can fulfil their needs. Princes maintain their throne if they cater to the needs of their subjects. When those needs are met, people support the Prince. Even in difficult circumstances, they become the biggest shield of the Prince. However, when the Prince is not able to satisfy the subjects, resentment follows. When the resentment is managed through persuasion, it is kept under control. But if the Prince becomes authoritarian to tackle the resentment, then a vicious cycle is unleashed, where Sages emerge, which leads to dethroning. Despite the pain of dethroning and a gruelling transition method, the Sage would always be driven by an ideology and the end goal.

Leading a society is always a great responsibility. If the so called Sage is driven by personal agenda, then power is bound to corrupt. They will ignore their subjects and become another Prince. In such situations, power may remain temporarily with them, but it inevitably departs in eventful circumstances. In the olden days, we often used to see people migrating out of treacherous systems rather than agitating. However, the presence of hard borders nowadays makes it difficult for people to migrate out. This makes the unjust regimes more susceptible to protests, civil wars and revolutions.

If someone is not driven by selflessness, power should be avoided. They should remain a Slave and never vie for power. Though it is understood, there will always be people among us who will pursue power for their personal gains. Such people claim incumbency and remain there for their personal agenda. Such people become Prince and use authoritarian power rather than influence, which keeps the door open for a Sage to dethrone them.

So, keeping the just needs of the Sage in mind, we can put six broad categories of goals. Each goal has its own dynamics and requires a different pathway and toppling method.

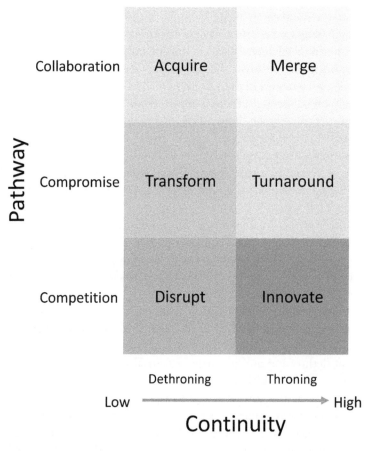

Figure 18.1 Goal of Sage.

Disruption is a goal pursued when interrupting the system is a necessity. The system is so diabolic that continuing it is no longer a possibility. The system needs a reset, and a new social order is the requirement. Such systems are dismantled, and a new order is created through adopting competitive pathway. The rise of the Communist Party in China is a good example of disruption. China was the 'Sick Man of Asia' facing social, economic and political upheaval. It led communists to join hands to take down the nationalist government completely in 1949. The result was the creation of the People's Republic of China, which is separate from the Republic of China (Taiwan).

Innovation is a goal when similar circumstances prevail as disruption, but instead of developing an ad hoc mechanism, power is erected from within the system. The challenger pursues a competitive spirit and proclaims leadership to innovate the system. The new system works for the betterment of the people, which allows the power to thrive. China, even after the disruption of 1949, was still struggling. So, Deng Xiaoping set aside many of Mao Zedong's policies. This paved the way for reformation, which allowed China to innovate its way to become a global leader.

Notice that both Mao and Deng were pursuing competition. Both had people's agendas on their mind. Both set aside the social order of the Prince. However, Mao came through revolution while Deng came from within the Communist Party. Mao disrupted the status quo while Deng innovated it into a new China.

Transformation is the goal when the system has lagged behind others. The Prince is not observing the outside world, which makes it noncompliant with the needs of the people. In such situations, the intention is to transform the rotting system so that it can thrive. Mustafa Kamal Ataturk became the first president of Turkey after he dethroned the Ottoman Sultan and various other contesting factions. To achieve the independence of Turkey, he compromised with the Allied forces and let go of many areas under Ottoman control. After independence, he transformed Turkey into a modern secular state from an Islamic Sultanate. His plans pivoted on six principles commonly known as six arrows.

The *turnaround* agenda meanwhile is pursued through the throning process. Here, continuity of the system is maintained while succeeding the existing power structure. The idea is to turn the system around to achieve its past glory by making changes to the current social order. Recep Tayyip Erdogan claimed premiership of Turkey in 2003. He was barred from contesting elections for five years in 1998 for reading an inflammatory poem. He contested his conviction but was unsuccessful. Instead of agitating, he compromised with the orders of the court. When he became eligible, he became prime minister and later president. He is now leading a turnaround agenda in Turkey. His ambition is to resurrect the glory days of the Ottoman Caliphate.

Both Ataturk and Erdogan rose to power in Turkey, eight decades apart. Both made compromises while becoming the leader of a nation. However, Ataturk dismantled the status quo and started it from scratch, while Erdogan used existing democratic practices to reach the top.

Acquisition is a goal pursued by people who display collaboration paths. They analyse a system that is weak. They lend their cooperating hand in a win–win situation. However, they use dethroning mechanisms to achieve this purpose. An example of this goal was seen when East India Company was on the verge of bankruptcy. The UK nationalized it in 1858, and all its customers were guaranteed a dividend. The acquisition allowed the UK to take over the company's Indian assets while the East India Company shareholders got redemption on their shares. A win-win situation emerged for both UK and East India Company shareholders.

A *merger* is a goal when the continuity of the system is prioritized. Collaboration mechanisms are used to combine the hands of all parties. The British East India Company used to offer the subsidiary alliance model to many principalities in India. The subsidiary alliance would enable the Maharaja to keep his domestic rule while paying tax to the company. In return, the principality was getting defence assurances. This arrangement avoided bloodshed and battles. The East India Company was anyways annihilating all local armies and annexing any territories that did not agree with the alliance model. Thus, the subsidiary alliance was a win–win for both the Maharaja and the East India Company.

Notice the subtle differences between the acquisition and merger. East India Company was in throning mode when it rolled out the subsidiary alliance model. Though the local Maharajas kept their rule but East India Company gained a significant piece of land and revenue. But nationalization of East India Company was a dethroning goal, which allowed the UK to exercise its power over East India Company and absorb its assets within the UK empire completely.

Looking back at Alexander's conquest of Persia, we notice that Alexander allowed many Persians in high-ranking positions after the conquest. He even allowed Persian culture to thrive. He was collaborative in his attitude. He even married a Persian princess Roxanna to promote interfaith harmony. This makes us believe that his goal was acquisition where he was more possessed with erecting a great multi-ethnic and multi-cultural empire spanning from West to East.

In the business world, corporations also work on these broad-based motives. These goals form the overarching goals from which different key performance indicators are derived. When the Google search engine came, it was not disrupting how search is conducted. It was merely innovating, as other players like Microsoft and Yahoo were there in the market to serve the needs of customers. Google innovated a new method, which allowed it to topple the incumbents. But the emergence of generative AI such as ChatGPT is a disruption. It has combined both information and write up in one place in an interactive format. It is trying to change the rule book on how search is consumed. So, in the same industry, we first saw Google innovation and now we are witnessing ChatGPT disruption.

So, based on these broad goals, the Sage should also develop their ideology when challenging the Prince. Without a goal and an ideology, a Sage is just another Prince who is consumed by power than by the betterment of people.

Part V

POWER AND MORALITY

Chapter 19

A MEASURE OF MORALITY

The measure of a man is what he does with power.

Pittacus

Nader Shah proclaimed power by becoming the Shah of Iran in 1736. He then led a military conquest towards Delhi in 1739. Despite being outnumbered, he humbled the Mughal emperor – Muhammad Shah. Midway through the surrender of Delhi, a rumour broke out that Nader is assassinated. This led many locals to agitate and brutalize the soldiers of the invading army. By the time Nader's army wrestled back control, over a thousand soldiers were killed. When Nader came to know about this, he reacted furiously and ordered his army to sack the city. Thousands of Delhiites were butchered in the ensuing mass looting. The brutal actions of Nader are heavily criticized in history, but he justified his actions by pointing towards the death of his comrades. He believed his actions were a retaliation to the action of the Delhiites. So, should we look at his justification? Or should we call Nader an immoral being for the genocide? It is often said that power is the measure of morality. One's values get displayed when they are in power. Nader's action to kill the Delhiites from the position of power also highlights his morality. But is power really the right measure to gauge someone?

Many thinkers, especially Greek philosophers, put a high emphasis on morality. They believe that morality is what drives human societies. They opine that morality is the perfect prism to gauge people in power. However, when we keenly look at morality, we observe it is a subjective phenomenon. There are no set standards of morality. Varying moral theories gauge actions differently. Some of these theories are listed below to highlight the element of subjectivity.

1. *Consequentialism* is when actions are gauged based on their consequences. If any action results in a good outcome, then the action is deemed moral. For instance, the extrajudicial killing of a murderer is a moral thing to do in consequentialism. Eliminating a murderer is beneficial to society as it eradicates the nuisance. So, should we call it a moral act?

2. *Deontology* is a moral theory that does not look at consequences but gauges actions from the prism of maintaining the honour and dignity of others. Immanuel Kant is the biggest proponent of this moral theory. He believes that intent and motive behind an action are necessary to gauge actions. If we believe this theory, then no action can be gauged as moral or immoral, as the intent of an action remains hidden from the outside world.

3. *Virtue Ethics* is when actions are gauged based on virtues such as honesty, fairness, compassion and so on. These virtues develop the character of the individual, which is the key to morality. If we believe this theory, then retaliating to a rude behaviour becomes an immoral act as it does not appeal to the virtue of compassion. So, should we never retaliate?

We see there is no single theory that explains the standards of morality. Even if we trust one or all of these theories, then the other problem is that the façade of morality is not static and changes with time and culture. Actions deemed moral in one culture are deemed immoral in another. Similarly, some immoral actions today were moral a few centuries ago. So, we cannot gauge one's legacy through the prism of morality when the standards of morality are changing.

To explain this further, let us look at the rise of Adolf Hitler. He came to the helm of power on the back of massive popularity. He raised anti-Semitic slogans to appeal to common Germans. While the world called Hitler's anti-Jewish policy as immoral, the Germans of that era did not see it that way. They genuinely believed in Hitler's views which lifted him to the power corridors. Similarly, Narendra Modi is giving air to Islamophobia on the same lines as the anti-Semitic policy of Hitler. He is raising Hindutva slogans and marginalizing the Muslim community of India, which may seem immoral to many, but many Indians do not see it that way. That is why the public has lifted Modi to power. Most pre-World War 2 Germans and today's Indians do not see religious hatred as immoral. They see no harm in marginalizing any community. So, we notice that standards of morality vary with cultures.

Similarly, we notice that standards of morality differ with time too. For example, killing a defeated soldier in the war is immoral now. There are treaties like the Geneva Convention to stop this from happening. However, it was a moral thing to do a few centuries ago. In Japan, helping to kill a defeated soldier was customary as part of the 'Seppuku' and 'Harakiri' tradition. So, the standards of morality change not only with culture but also with time.

The third, more complicated issue with using morality as a gauge is the fixed 'Frame of Reference'. A frame of reference is the concept of gauging someone's actions by discounting the circumstances and looking at actions in isolation. To explain the concept of the frame of reference, let us take the example of a mugger holding a gun to our head. He is flexing his power authorized by the gun in his hand. He exercises his power over us by demanding our wallet. If we do what he wants us to do, then we go free. Alternatively, he can shoot us in the head. Knowing this, we hand over our wallet to him. If we end the discussion here, then we agree that power is a measure of morality. If the mugger had no power, then he would not have mugged us. The mugger's immoral values get displayed when he got power. So, power became an enabler to display his immoral values. However, when we place a broader frame of reference to include the mugger's circumstances, then the situation changes. It is possible that the mugger's act is triggered due to desperation for money. He may have been neglected by the government in developing his skills to earn a decent livelihood. This may have forced him to weaponize himself and mug people. So, while we may be calling the mugger immoral, he may have been a victim of the government's unfair socio-economic policy. We then must look at the mugger from the victim's lens rather than the aggressor's lens. The mugger may be using his power to repel the social injustice done to him, which is in retaliation to the government's policies. Since retaliation does not qualify as immoral, these details do not make his actions immoral. Notice these details emerge when we broaden the frame of reference. Now, if we focus on the government in this episode and start calling it immoral for leaving behind a citizen, it may have also been a victim to a corporate lobby. The corporate lobby might have forced the government to reduce taxes, which stopped the government from spending money on developing the mugger into a responsible citizen. In this case, the government becomes a victim rather than an aggressor. If we move to the corporate lobby, they too may have been a victim to someone's aggression. So, the lens between the victim and the aggressor keeps on changing depending on when we place our frame of reference. If our frame of reference is the interaction between the mugger and the victim, then we can safely say that the use of power is a measure of morality. But if we expand our frame of reference to include the government and the corporate lobby, then this conclusion of marking the mugger as immoral goes out of the window.

To conclude the above example, when we expand our frame of reference, the mugger may come out clean as he may have used power in self-defence, which complies with any standards of morality. Similarly, the government and the corporate lobby may also come clean as they may have also been using their power in self-defence. So, to mark power as a measure of morality is only applicable when it is applied to a very narrow frame of reference. As soon as we broaden the horizon of the reference point, the whole conclusion crumbles.

If we look at some real-life examples, the fallacy of frame of reference becomes even more clear. When we observe the US war on terror and use a narrow time frame of 2009, when the United States started drone strikes to kill Al Qaeda members, then, we conclude that the US military was immoral. The US military was using its power to wage an offensive in Afghanistan but killed many innocent Afghans in collateral damage. If we constrain our frame of reference here, we can safely say that the US military is immoral. But when we expand our reference frame to include the tragedy of 9/11, we know that the US military was acting in self-defence to eliminate terrorism hotspots in pre-emptive strikes. Based on this, it becomes questionable to call the US military immoral. We can call their drone policy wrong, but we cannot call their actions immoral. Similarly, if we look at the legendary life of Nelson Mandela, we get to know that he was leading an armed struggle against the government. He was on a rampage to sabotage the government. If we use the narrow frame of the early life of Mandela, his acts do not comply with morality as he became a nuisance to South African government. His early life was reminiscent of terrorists. Will we then conclude that Mandela was an immoral being? However, all his actions were a retaliation to the apartheid regime, which raised awareness among marginalized communities. If we look at Saddam Hussein, we see him using his power in a tyrannical way. He pinned down his opposition and, in many cases, butchered them. We celebrated his capture, and no one shed a tear when he was hanged, as we believe that he was immoral. But we conveniently forget that his oppression on Iraqis contained the nemesis of ISIS. He succeeded in snubbing the extremist views prevailing in that region. Once Saddam was toppled, ISIS proclaimed itself and manifested their insane ideology in the region. If we use a narrow frame in each of these three examples, then the US military was immoral as it killed Afghans, Mandela was immoral as he sabotaged government properties and Saddam was immoral as he allowed no civil liberties. But when we expand our references, then we get to know that the US military was trying to eliminate terrorism, Mandela was fighting for social equality and Saddam was snubbing an extremist mindset. All these actions are not immoral by any standards.

One may question here that the above examples have ad hominem and whataboutism associated with them. Individual circumstances do not warrant anyone to become an aggressor. While whataboutism, tu quoque and ad-hominem are hypocritical ways to defend a position, these techniques are widely used in daily arguments. Many actions of powerful people are triggered due to the maxim of ad hominem debating technique. They satisfy their conscious by invoking their circumstances. In the case of Nader too, his circumstances triggered his reaction. He ordered the genocide after his soldiers were killed. So, his defence relies on the same principle of whata-boutism. Meanwhile, the observer's judgement is based on a fixed frame of reference of looking at mass murders of Delhiites. If both Nader and observ-ers keep on holding their viewpoint, then we will never be able to conclude the debate on morality.

The ideal-type fallacy is the fourth problem with using power as a stand-ard for morality. In the ideal type, one superimposes their own standards to judge others. In the case of a mugger, one may say that mugging is immoral based on their own ideal type. The mugger may point out that someone else's moral standards are forced upon them when judging his actions.

So based on the above discussion, it becomes impossible to use morality as a gauge because, (1) there is no consensus on what constitutes moral actions, (2) the standards of morality evolve with time and culture, (3) the fluidity of the frame of references and (4) the ideal-type fallacy. Added to this complex-ity is that sometimes power demands tough decisions. Tough decisions often result in victims. Hence, if we continue to use power as a basis to judge moral-ity, then most people will fail this test. We will end up calling every Sage immoral, which will leave us with no dividing line between Prince and Sage. Therefore, we must look elsewhere to judge Sage, as morality alone does not conclude the debate.

However, if we look at drawing a line from the angle of authority and influ-ence, it leads to an answer. Power is derived from both authority and influ-ence. Unlike morality, these two factors eliminate subjectivity as it is easier to assess the sources of power. If power is derived from authority alone, then the person may delve into a Prince mode, but if power is derived from influence, then even the most immoral acts may become an act of Sage. To explain this subtle difference, let us look at the above examples again and pass them through the prism of authority and influence to judge if this is indeed the case. The mugger is deriving his power from the authority given to him by the gun. The US military bombed Afghans out of authority vested by the UN charter, which allows self-defence, Mandela was deriving influence from Black South Africans by sabotaging apartheid policies and Saddam was deriving his inhu-man actions from the government machinery. Now when we segregate all these seemingly immoral actions based on authority and influence, then we get to know that Mandela was influential in his actions while the mugger, US military and Saddam were authoritarian in their proceedings. That is why we can call Mandela a Sage while we condemn the actions of the mugger, the US military and Saddam.

To explain this differentiation further, let us assume that a company is going through organizational changes and used its discretionary powers to fire an employee. If we use the veil of morality, this action seems immoral. Mere

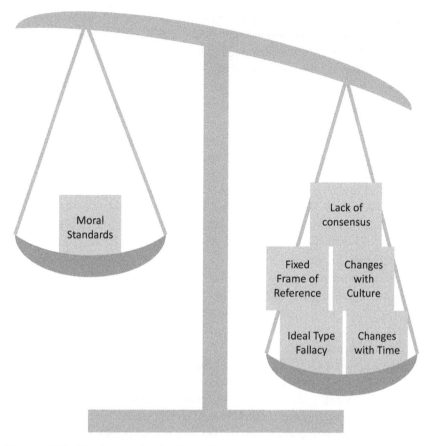

Figure 19.1 Varying standards of morality.

restructuring does not warrant laying off an employee. But when we change the frame of reference, and the audience learns that the fired employee was a sexual predator, the same immoral act becomes an act of leadership. We then must applaud the policies of the company. But let us say we get to know that the employee was fired because of whistleblowing the dishonest practices of the company, then the same act of firing becomes an act of cruelty. In the former scenario, the company derives its decision from visionary influence, where its vision is zero tolerance towards harassment. In the latter scenario, the company derives its decisions from incentive authority, where the incentive is to exchange employment with silence. So, the same action of firing, which is immoral, reveals two different versions when we pass it through the prism of authority and influence. The implication of the decision becomes obvious. That is why power needs to be gauged through the lens of authority and influence rather than the veil of morality.

When we look at the orders of Nader to plunder Delhi through the prism of authority and influence, we see that he gained authority as a conqueror. He harnessed tremendous power by inflicting fear in the minds of people but gained little influence through marching in the city. When he allowed the looting and plundering, he was not deriving any influence but was using the authority bestowed on him as a victor of the invading army. If we use the prism of morality on Nader, he could go unblemished by invoking the deaths of his comrades as a reason for his reaction. But when we look at the incident from the lens of authority and influence, we know that his purging orders were authoritarian, due to which we will always condemn his actions.

The real-life example of Steve Jobs is another way to understand influence and authority. Steve Jobs was famous for using rowdy behaviour among his colleagues. Many of his friends were victims of his cutthroat policies. If we gauge Jobs' legacy behind the veil of morality, then he may not get a favourable opinion. But when we see his legacy through the prism of authority and influence, then we get to know how he became such a successful leader. Many of his tough decisions were taken from his authority as the CEO of Apple, but he was influencing the masses through leading the development of blockbuster products. His power was derived from both authority and influence, but he garnered more influence among the public than authority from his corporate position. Therefore, Jobs is remembered as a legendary figure.

To conclude this discussion, we should re-think our approach to gauge power through morality lens. We should rather use authority and influence to gauge power.

Chapter 20

WHEN POWER BECOMES EVIL

Power ought to serve as a check to power.

Montesquieu

Equatorial Guinea was a Spanish colony until 1969. Before becoming an independent country, elections were conducted in 1968 under Spanish supervision to transition power to the local leadership. Francisco Macias Nguema won the mandate and later became president of independent Equatorial Guinea. Once the Spaniards left, Nguema ditched his democratic tendencies and consolidated power at the top. In his first move, he executed the runner-up of the presidential election – Ondu Edu. He then purged his opponents one by one and later banned all political parties so that no one could challenge him. He proclaimed absolute power in 1973 when he banned democracy altogether. After proclaiming dictatorship, he butchered anyone whose loyalty was questionable. However, when he questioned the allegiance of his own family members, his nephew – Teodoro Mbasogo – toppled him. Mbasogo took power in 1979 and spared no mercy for his uncle. After a show trial, Nguema was executed by a firing squad. However, the change of guard in Equatorial Guinea brought no respite for the common (wo)man. Mbasogo is as authoritarian as his uncle was. So, what led democracy to yield a brutal dictator like Nguema? How does power evolve into an evil phenomenon in some societies?

Power is often considered a taboo. Some associate voodoo with it, and others with virtue. However, it is a neutral phenomenon. It is like fire, which, if controlled, keeps us warm during winter, but if uncontrolled, torches up the whole house. Similarly, power can help maintain peace and is a source of binding people if used properly, but it can also trigger a world war if left unchecked. It is a shallow view to look upon power in a negative light. However, merely looking at de jure understanding of power does not complete the discussion, as many people associate power with cruelty and tyranny. We must develop a model when power becomes evil and an uncontrollable feature.

The core reason that power becomes tyrannical is not that it is an evil phenomenon per se but because it is immeasurable. No one can claim to know how much power they possess. Power is not a tangible phenomenon like money which can be counted. Power is the summation of influence and authority. In many parts of the world, conventional and rational authority are measurable as they are sanctioned by law or a third party, which define the boundaries of power. But other forms of authority – charismatic and incentive – are not clearly defined, which leads to the confusion on how much authority one has. Similarly, both kinds of influence – visionary and relational – are immeasurable. Influence is a fluid phenomenon anyways which keeps on evolving depending on the relation between the power and the subject. Thus, the uncertainty revolving around influence and authority makes power immeasurable. However, if someone is deriving power from conventional or rational authority like a tribal chief and a police(wo)man, then we can determine the quantum of power.

Now that we have established that power cannot be assessed easily, let us look at it from a psychological point of view. Because of the uncertainty around the quantum of power, people usually underestimate it. They perceive their power to be lower than they possess, making them insecure. They feel that their power quotient is inadequate to fulfil their needs independently. Recall that in previous chapters we have established that those who pursue power are Sages and Princes. Sages have little needs; hence, they have no insecurity. But Princes prioritize needs. So, when Princes believe that their needs cannot be fulfilled with the quantum of power they possess, they fall prey to an inferiority complex. They initially start consolidating power through authority or influence to ensure that their urgent needs are not in any imminent danger. They harness power for defensive purposes at this stage. This is exactly the rationale presented by Realists who justify the accumulation of power as necessary to defend themselves. The defensive power is not questioned as people remain harmless with this power. But a time arrives when a constant accumulation of power allows Princes to fulfil their higher needs. These needs are in the shape of recognition and self-esteem. They then prioritize their ego and individualism over the collective good of society. This inevitably pits them against Sages who stand for the interests of the society. Princes then go on a rampage to eliminate those who become a hurdle. At this stage, defensive power morphs into aggressive power in the form of authority and dictation. When we analyse what is the root cause of such power, it comes out that it is the insecurity of a Prince. Princes' inferiority complex initially leads them to accumulate power and then trigger a wave of tyranny.

The tipping point of defensive power morphing into aggressive power is the unification of all dimensions of power. We know that power has three facets – Decision, Non-decision and Opinion control. Princes' journey usually starts with one dimension, but when all dimensions of power are consolidated, then it becomes totalitarian power. This is the power that is tyrannical and evil. So, if power remains defensive, then it is not harmful. But, when it becomes offensive, it becomes questionable. Famous writers like George Orwell, who ridiculed power in their writings, see power when it has become aggressive and totalitarian. The core reason of totalitarian power is inferiority complex which forces Princes to keep harnessing more power to ensure their freedom and survival. If we look around history, we will notice all kinds of evil power showing signs of (1) insecurity followed by (2) power accumulation and ending with (3) unification of all dimensions of power.

To stop the evil ingress of power, the onus lies on society. They must ensure that the person in power either (a) does not accumulate as much power to become aggressive or (b) remains insecure throughout their reign. The method to achieve this is to ensure that at least one powerful Sage remains in society. Sages function as a deterrent to Princes. The prevalence of a Prince and a Sage in a society ensures that the Prince is facing an opposition. However, if these two fail-safe switches to stem a Prince fail, then power morphs into aggression and abuse.

The famous philosopher Montesquieu hypothesized his separation of power theory based on the first fail-safe switch. He believes separation of power is the only way to stop abusive and oppressive power. So, mechanisms need to be put in place to stop the consolidation of power on one hand. Another philosopher, Hannah Arendt, requests people to adopt natality which refers to the human collective actions to bring about change. She is talking about the second fail-safe mechanism to stop the ingress of evil power. She is of the view that there should exist a resistance in society, which thwarts any aggression of totalitarian and Princely power.

To explain the evil evolution of power and how society can function as a deterrent, let us relook at the case of the mugger snatching the wallet. But this time, we will take four scenarios to explain how evil power progresses and how it is stopped. We know that the mugger belongs to the Prince category where he prioritizes the fulfilment of his need independently. Recall from previous chapters that prioritizing needs without independence makes the mugger a beggar. So, all muggers fall into the Prince category where the intent is to keep the fulfilment of needs in their own hands.

In the first scenario, the mugger does not have a gun. He does not have enough power on his own. He fears he cannot simply walk to the victim demanding their wallet. Without the gun, the mugger perceives his power to be inadequate to force a thuggery. He may use his power to defend himself but cannot use it for aggression. Since defensive power is invisible, society does not witness the restraint shown by the mugger when he does not snatch the wallet. In this scenario, the victim walks past him with no snatching episode. Notice that the need of the mugger was still there, but the power quotient was not enough to snatch the wallet.

In the second scenario, let us say that the same mugger's insecurity led him to accumulate power. He harnesses additional power by buying a gun. The total quantum of power the mugger possesses with the gun goes higher than without the gun. He believes that now he can snatch the victim's wallet. He can independently fulfil his need through the power quotient he possesses. The mugger moves forward and points the gun at the victim, giving no option to the victim other than handing over the wallet. Any resistance shown by the victim may result in murder. So, the victim hands over the wallet, and the mugger shows the dark side of power. All conditions of evil power are satisfied in this scenario. The insecurity led to power accumulation through the gun, and unification happened when no option is given to the victim other than handing over the wallet. Power in this scenario becomes evil. Notice that if the mugger was without a gun, he used power for defence. But as soon as he harnessed enough power through the gun, power became offensive. In the first scenario, power was invisible as it was defensive, but in the second scenario, power is visible as it is aggressive.

In the above two scenarios, the victim is assumed to be from the Slave category. He shows no retaliation. But let us assume that the victim is a Sage. The victim knows how to showcase his freedom. Now, let us imagine a third scenario where the Sage victim is pinned against the Prince mugger with a gun. The victim has been trained methodically in how to tackle guns. The power of the victim is based on mastering the art of disarming aggressors. Without gauging the victim's power, the mugger assaults. At this stage, the mugger uses aggressive power while the victim is using defensive power. The victim retaliates. Since the victim is trained to manage these kinds of situations, he disarms the mugger. The victim wins, and the mugger ends up in jail or runs away. In this scenario, the first two conditions of evil power are satisfied, but the third does not happen as the victim thwarts the mugger. We see aggressive power in this scenario too, but power does not become tyrannical as it is nipped in the bud. The first fail switch works where the mugger has not accumulated as much power to pin the Sage victim.

Now let us complicate the situation even further by introducing a fourth scenario. Let us assume that the victim showcases his martial arts skills in a street performance. The same mugger is also in the audience and later notices the victim walking alone in the dark. The mugger acknowledges that the victim has the capability and capacity to subdue him. So, in this scenario, the mugger will let the victim pass and hunt for another victim that night. In this scenario, we do not see aggressive power as power does not become tyrannical. The second fail-safe switch works where the victim makes the mugger insecure.

Notice that in Scenario 3, the first fail-safe switch stems from aggressive power. The mugger could not unify all dimensions of power. In Scenario 4, the second fail-safe switch works. The victim forces the mugger to remain defensive by showcasing his own power. The victim's display of defensive power is adequate to thwart the evil designs of the mugger. So, these two fail-safe switches are mechanisms to stop the abusive wave of power in any society.

When we look at Nguema, he was also a proponent of evil power. He grew up in a troubled childhood and witnessed the colonial might of Spain's dictatorial regime led by Francisco Franco. The circumstances around him made him insecure. Instead of standing up to the colonial powers, he became a Slave. He knew that his needs depended on staying closer to power circles. But when Spaniards were leaving the country, he campaigned aggressively for elections to get a grip on power. He wanted to stay relevant in post-colonial

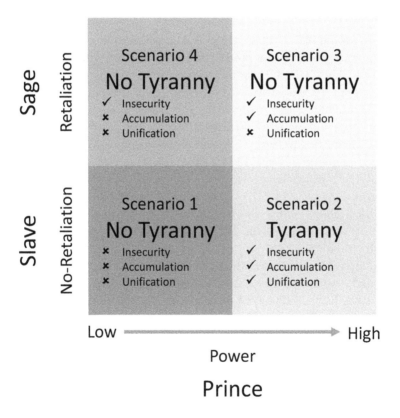

Figure 20.1 Power becoming evil.

Equatorial Guinea to keep satisfying his needs. Once he won the elections, the presidential authority gave him the initial impetus needed to consolidate power. He murdered his challenger and purged all his opponents. In 1973, Nguema passed an act to outlaw any political activity where he unified all dimensions of power. So, all three conditions of evil power became true. But both fail-safe switches to control tyrannical power malfunctioned. Had Edu remained alive to keep threatening Nguema or the public had protested the concentration of power on one hand, things could have been different in Equatorial Guinea. The same fail-safe switches malfunctioned again when Mbasogo took over in 1979.

One may notice that consolidation of power is not in the hands of subjects, but retaliation is. The bad name of power, on one hand, is by people with an inferiority complex, but on the other hand, by society not rising to aggression. The brutal and gruesome regimes usually prevail in a society composed of Slaves. In these societies, Princes have a free pass to exercise their actions as no one challenges them. In such societies where Princes are consolidating power, empowering a Sage is obligatory. The evil power is associated with powerful people not fearing a retaliation.

There are numerous examples of war generals falling for the same fallacy where they believed that their conquest would be swift with little-to-no retaliation. They believed that their opposition had a Slave mentality. The events leading to World War 1 are reminiscent of this fallacy. Archduke Franz Ferdinand of the Austria-Hungary Empire was assassinated by a Serb in 1914. Taking this event as an excuse, Germans wanted Austro-Hungarians to declare war on Serbia immediately as they believed they were well prepared to wage an offensive. Germans were left behind in the colonial race, which triggered their inferiority complex. However, they undermined the resistance they would face. When the war began, Germans found themselves resisted vehemently by France, which ended up in the Treaty of Versailles. So, the ingress of aggressive power was stemmed through retaliation.

Similarly, Adolf Hitler was the victim of the same fallacy in World War 2. Hitler had developed an inferiority complex after the humiliation of World War 1, so he harnessed power both domestically and internationally. Hitler had assurances from the USSR through the Molotov-Ribbentrop Pact, which led him to believe that he would face little resistance. He greatly underestimated the involvement of France and the UK. In the initial periods of war, his gamble to control Europe almost paid off until the Soviets and the United States both jumped in the European theatre and turned the table.

The US theatrics in Vietnam and Afghanistan are also examples of the same fallacy. In both cases, the United States believed that they could take over Viet Cong and Taliban swiftly. However, the US military might was resisted ferociously and humbled where the world witnessed the chaos unravelling after the fall of Saigon and Kabul.

To sum up, if any power becomes aggressive or shows its uncontrollable nature, it should be retaliated. The onus lies on the society to empower a Sage in these circumstances to disrupt the power from becoming evil.

Chapter 21

THE DARK TETRAD

Power doesn't corrupt people, people corrupt power.

William Gaddis

Vlad III, commonly called Vlad the Impaler, was the voivode of Wallachia, present-day Romania. He claimed the throne under eventful circumstances in 1456. After claiming the throne, he unravelled a tale of atrocities. He devised a brutal way of impaling his opponents on stakes and leaving them to die slowly. Wallachia acted as a buffer state between Hungary and the Ottomans. Vlad tried to break free from this arrangement, which pitted him against the might of Sultan Mehmed II. When the Ottoman army started their march towards Targovishte, Vlad adopted a scorched-earth policy. He burnt all fields and poisoned all water resources in their path to deprive them of food. He then devised a hit-and-run method to stem the march of the invaders. Despite all these tactics, the Ottomans finally reached the capital city and took Targovishte. However, Vlad left behind a trail of impaled bodies. When Mehmed entered the fort, he was horrified by the brutal scenes. Looking at this event, we can notice that Vlad's cruelty knew no bounds. Keeping his brutality in mind, can we develop a parameter on what type of characters are prone to becoming evil? Is ideology and deriving influence the only criteria to become a Sage or do we have any other criteria to isolate barbaric characters who display an ideology?

To understand the toxicity of most likely people who abuse power, we must first understand the dark triad. Dark triad is a concept popularized by Delroy Paulhus and Kevin Williams. It is a combination of three personality traits: Machiavellianism, narcissism and psychopathy. Each trait displays a dark behaviour of an individual, which later becomes a source of brutality and violence. A short description of each is below.

Machiavellianism is a behaviour dominated by deceit and cunningness. This behaviour is named after the famous Italian philosopher Niccolo Machiavelli. He is often credited for preaching dubious methods to serve an individual agenda. People displaying Machiavellianism have higher levels of intelligence, allowing them to mould themselves according to the situation. They display no ideology but show pragmatism in the eye of a challenge. They serve their own selfish agenda, paying no heed to rules or methods to achieve it. The antagonist of this book – Prince – is a Machiavellian.

Narcissism is a behaviour dominated by grandiosity and entitlement. These people have an innate sense of superiority which becomes a source of abnormal behaviour. They are often self-absorbed people with a high sense of ego. Their sole goal is to claim accolades from others, often at the expense of others. Though deep down, they are insecure, which makes them defensive. They deflect blame on others to give a boost to their inflated self-esteem.

Psychopathy is often used interchangeably with sociopathy. A lack of emotions and compassion defines this trait. Psychopaths often display callous and self-serving behaviour with no remorse or regret. They show coldness and arrogance in their daily life. They are not afraid to take any action, even if it harms others. An extreme case of psychopathy turns violent and displays criminal tendencies.

A fourth trait, Sadism, is often missed out of the dark triad. Sadism involves getting pleasure out of inflicting pain on others. This trait, along with the other three, makes it a dark tetrad. Sadism is increasingly associated with dominating behaviour in sexual acts, but it has connotations to everyday life as well. A sadistic personality derives joy from dominating and exerting control over others. Their cruelty can be verbal or physical.

When we look at Vlad's wave of terror, we see signs of sadism. In his childhood, Vlad and his brother Radu were held captive by Ottomans to secure their father's loyalty. Despite this, their father switched his allegiance leaving him at the mercy of Sultan Murad. Though Murad spared Vlad's life, he grew up in a sad environment away from his family and estate. He saw the dominance of the Ottomans, which may have developed his sadistic tendencies. When he proclaimed himself as the voivode of Wallachia, he inflicted gruesome pain on his opponents. He did not give an easy death to his victims. When he was confronted with Mehmed, he resorted to the scorch-earth policy. He burnt fields of his own country(wo)men where he showed no compassion for anyone. All his efforts were directed at inflicting pain on others. Unsurprisingly, he is remembered as an Impaler rather than a benevolent ruler.

One may question whether it is unfair to judge Vlad as sadistic? After all, most rulers of that era showed signs of cruelty and barbarism. The answer is that all humans are born with some level of dark traits. However, the extent of these traits varies. A lower level of dark behaviour does not pose any harm to society. It is managed and remains within an individual's psychology. It is the extreme cases of machiavellianism, narcissism, psychopathy and sadism

Psychopathy   Narcissism

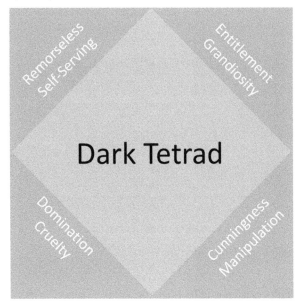

Sadism   Machiavellianism

Figure 21.1 Dark tetrad model.

which are disturbing. Those displaying outright dark traits, such as Vlad, turn barbaric when tested with power.

The Sage may also have these dark traits but these traits do not define them. They learn the art of coming out of any dark behaviour which allows them to stay true to their ideals. Fascists like Hitler who indeed displayed an ideology get filtered out from Sage criteria based on this segregation. To emerge as a Sage, one has to overcome the machiavellian, narcissistic, psychopathic and sadistic tendencies. Hitler displayed extreme forms of sadism which qualifies him as a fascist dictator but not as a Sage. Society also has to be careful of these traits before empowering a Sage to take down a Prince.

To segregate people with dark behaviour even before they proclaim power, we must assess them on the Five Factor Model. The model tests people on Openness, Conscientiousness, Extraversion, Agreeableness and Neuroticism or simply OCEAN. The test gives an overarching view of an individual's personality, which may become a leading indicator in judging if the person in power will become cruel and oppressive.

One common thing between all people showing dark traits is their low level of agreeableness. They are non-cooperative. They do not entertain any

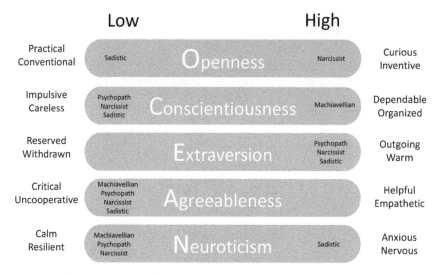

Figure 21.2 Ocean model for leadership.

opposite view. An argument with them inevitably becomes ugly. A psychopath usually invokes ridicule when confronted, a narcissist turns defensive, a machiavellian resorts to whataboutism and sadist intimidates others. Another key feature in the life of dark personalities is a lack of empathy. They do not care about others and are driven by their own needs. Recall that a Prince, too, has high needs, and so do these four dark personalities. So, anyone showing low agreeableness and lack of empathy is likely to be a Prince and turn evil.

Many people may confuse a low level of agreeableness with Sages as well. When a Slave turns into a Sage, other members of society may try to pull them back to Slavery through peer pressure or some other social influence. They may appear naïve and stubborn when they pursue an ideology. However, low needs and high independence drive Sages which forces them to remain true to their ideology than to their ego. So, the best way is to look at their empathetic and socialist nature. That way, members of the society can assess if the candidate is going to be a Sage or a Prince.

On the same line, the corporate world also needs to develop empathetic tendencies. Cutthroat corporate cultures are paving the way for machiavellians, narcissists, psychopaths and sadists to flourish. These policies are increasingly allowing people with dark personality disorder to make progress and rise the corporate ladder. It is high time that corporations infuse empathy into their working culture and promote employees who display cooperation than competition and callousness. Otherwise, we will keep seeing a higher ratio of CEOs and executive leadership displaying dark behaviours, which will compound corporate greed.

BIBLIOGRAPHY

Acemoglu, D., and J. A. Robinson. 2012. *Why Nations Fail: The Origins of Power, Prosperity, and Poverty*. Currency.

Afkhami, Gholam R. 2009. *The Life and Times of the Shah*. University of California Press.

Allison, G. 2018. *Destined For War: Can America and China Escape Thucydides's Trap?* Mariner Books.

Aquinas, T. 2018. *Summa Theologica*. Coyote Canyon Press.

Arendt, H. 1973. *The Origins of Totalitarianism*. Harcourt, Brace, Jovanovich.

Bell, J. B. 1996. *Terror Out of Zion: Fight for Israeli Independence*. Routledge.

Booker, Christopher. 2005. *The Seven Basic Plots: Why We Tell Stories*. Continuum.

Bouverie, Tim. 2019. *Appeasement: Chamberlain, Hitler, Churchill, and the Road to War*. Tim Duggan Books.

Bray, Mark. 2013. *Translating Anarchy: The Anarchism of Occupy Wall Street*. Zero Books.

Brinkley, Douglas G. 2005. *Rosa Parks: A Life*. Penguin Books.

Budge, Ian, David Marsh, and David McKay. 1983. *The New British Political System: Government and Society in the 1980s*. Longman Publishing Group.

Burki, Shahid J. 1988. *Pakistan Under Bhutto, 1971–1977*. Palgrave Macmillan.

Coughlin, Con. 2005. *Saddam: His Rise and Fall*. Ecco.

Dahl, Robert A. 2005. *Who Governs?: Democracy And Power In An American City*. Yale University Press.

Deutsch, Karl W. 1963. *The Nerves of Government: Models of Political Communication and Control*. Free Press.

Franklin, R. L. 2018. *Freewill and Determinism: A Study of Rival Conceptions of Man*. Routledge.

Gandhi, Mahatma K. 2009. *The Story of My Experiments with Truth: An Autobiography*. Fingerprint! Publishing.

Gautheir, David P. 1979. *The Logic of Leviathan: The Moral and Political Theory of Thomas Hobbes*. Oxford University Press.

Gough, J. W. 1936. *The Social Contract – A Critical Study of Its Development*. Oxford at the Clarendon Press.

Henty, George A. 2019. *The Tiger of Mysore: A Story of the War with Tippoo Saib*. Wentworth Press.

Hibbert, Christopher. 2008. *Mussolini: The Rise and Fall of Il Duce: The Rise and Fall of Il Duce*. St. Martin's Griffin.

Huntington, S. P. 1996. *The Clash of Civilizations and the Remaking of World Order*. Simon & Schuster.

Jordan, A. G., and J. J. Richardson. 1987. *Government and Pressure Groups in Britain*. Oxford University Press.

Kant, I., and J. W. Ellington. 1993. *Grounding for the Metaphysics of Morals.* Hackett Publishing Company.

Kelman, Herbert C. 2018. *Herbert C. Kelman: A Pioneer in the Social Psychology of Conflict Analysis and Resolution.* Springer.

King, David. 2018. *The Trial of Adolf Hitler: The Beer Hall Putsch and the Rise of Nazi Germany.* W. W. Norton & Company.

Kirtzman, Andrew. 2022. *Giuliani: The Rise and Tragic Fall of America's Mayor.* Simon & Schuster.

Kwang, Han F., Warren Fernandez, and Sumiko Tan. 1998. *Lee Kuan Yew, the Man and His Ideas.* Times Editions.

Lebowitz, Michael A. 2009. *Following Marx: Method, Critique and Crisis.* Haymarket Books.

Leeming, David A. 1996. *A Dictionary of Creation Myths.* Oxford University Press.

Lenski, Gerhard. 2015. *Ecological-Evolutionary Theory: Principles and Applications.* Routledge.

Lukes, Steven. 2004. *Power: A Radical View.* Red Globe Press.

Mandela, Nelson. 1995. *A Long Walk to Freedom: The Autobiography of Nelson Mandela.* Time Warner Books UK.

Marx, Karl, and Friedrich Engels. 2014. *The Communist Manifesto.* International Publishers Company.

Maslow, Abraham H. 2013. *A Theory of Human Motivation.* Martino Fine Books.

McLynn, F. 2016. *Genghis Khan: His Conquests, His Empire, His Legacy.* Da Capo Press.

Meyer, G. J. 2010. *The Tudors: The Complete Story of England's Most Notorious Dynasty.* Delacorte Press.

Michels, Robert. 1966. *Political Parties: A Sociological Study of the Oligarchial Tendencies of Modern Democracy.* Free Press.

Mills, C. W., and Alan Wolfe. 2000. *The Power Elite.* Oxford University Press.

Montesquieu, C. 1989. *Montesquieu: The Spirit of the Laws.* Cambridge University Press.

Morgenthau, Hans. 2005. *Politics Among Nations: The Struggle for Power and Peace.* 7th ed. McGraw-Hill Education.

Mosca, Gaetano. 2015. *The Ruling Class.* Scholar's Choice.

Pareto, Vilfredo. 2015. *The Mind and Society <Trattato Di Sociologia Generale>.* Andesite Press.

Payne, R. 1965. *The Rise and Fall of Stalin.* Simon and Schuster.

Plato, and D. Gallop. 2009. *Phaedo.* Oxford University Press.

Popham, Peter. 2016. *The Lady and the Generals: Aung San Suu Kyi and Burma's Struggle for Freedom.* Rider.

Raphael, David D. 1987. *Political Thought and Its History: The Concept of Justice.* Department of Politics, The University of Sheffield.

Rawls, John. 2009. *A Theory of Justice.* Harvard University Press.

Ritter, Alan. 2015. *Political Thought of Pierre-Joseph Proudhon.* Princeton University Press.

Rosen, Allen D. 1996. *Kant's Theory of Justice.* Cornell University Press.

Sheinkin, Steve. 2010. *The Notorious Benedict Arnold: A True Story of Adventure, Heroism & Treachery.* Macmillan USA.

Smith, Brian K. 1994. *Classifying the Universe: The Ancient Indian Varna System and the Origins of Caste.* Oxford University Press.

Strathern, Paul. 2017. *The Medici: Power, Money, and Ambition in the Italian Renaissance.* Pegasus Books.

Tainter, J. A. 1990. *The Collapse of Complex Societies.* Cambridge University Press.

Thoreau, H. D. *Henry David Thoreau Collection: On the Duty of Civil Disobedience*. Independently Published.

Waldron, Jeremy. 2008. *God, Locke, and Equality: Christian Foundations in Locke's Political Thought*. Cambridge University Press.

Weber, Max. 2021. *Politics As a Vocation*. Hassell Street Press.

Wick, G. 2020. *The Dark Triad: The Dark Psychology Behind Narcissistic, Machiavellian and Psychopathic Behavior and Manipulation*. Independently Published.

Wraight, Christopher D. 2009. *Rousseau's 'The Social Contract': A Reader's Guide*. Continuum.

INDEX

Milton Keynes UK
Ingram Content Group UK Ltd.
UKHW010613020724
444982UK00016B/145